Bicycling

The Natchez Trace

A Guide to the Natchez Trace Parkway
and Nearby Scenic Routes

GLEN WANNER

3rd Edition

PENNYWELL PRESS

Edited by Ann Richards; Cover photography by Ed Wanner Cover design by Linda Nelson; Inside photography by Ann Richards, Glen Wanner, and the National Park Service.

Pennywell Press
P.O. Box 50624
Nashville, TN 37205

Distributed to book trade by John F. Blair Publisher, 1406 Plaza Dr. Winston-Salem, NC 27103
Publisher Cataloging Data
Wanner, Glen, 1964-
  Bicycling the Natchez Trace: A Guide to the Natchez Trace Parkway and Nearby Scenic Routes/ by Glen Wanner
  3rd Edition
  ISBN 0-9637798-6-9
  1. Bicycle Touring—Natchez Trace Parkway (MS, AL, and TN)—Guidebooks.
  2. Natchez Trace Parkway (MS, AL, and TN)—Description and travel—Guidebooks.
Printed by McNaughton & Gunn, Inc. Saline, MI

ACKNOWLEDGMENTS

I dedicate this book to my wife (and co-author of *Bicycling Middle Tennessee*) Ann Richards and our son Marcus who has graciously allowed me to tow him in his bike trailer for many miles on the Natchez Trace Parkway. May the rural roads we pedal—along with the forests and wild areas we enjoy—still be there for his and future generations.

Special thanks go to the friendly staff of the Natchez Trace Parkway, especially Sarah Leach and Leslie Blythe, for their assistance. On behalf of the many cyclists who pedal the Parkway, helmets off to all the Park Service personnel who frequently assist self-propelled travelers. Additional thanks to the local cyclists and bike shop owners who have shared their favorite routes with me.

I also wish to express my appreciation to those who have shared their expertise—Durwood Edwards for all kinds of computer help; Linda Nelson for her artistic eye and flair for design; my father Ed Wanner for his photographic talents; and Larry and Betty Richards for taking good care of Marcus.

TABLE OF CONTENTS

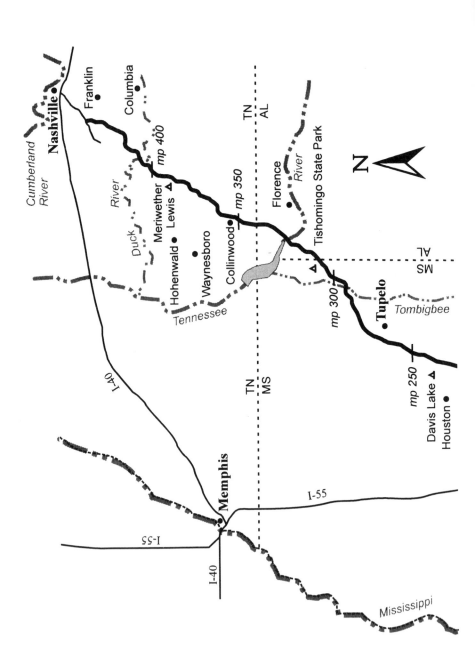

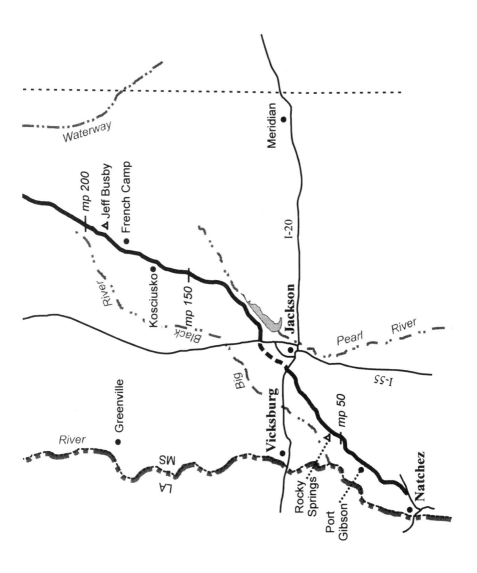

INTRODUCTION

Imagine a ribbon of pavement winding along forested ridges, broad valleys, and remote hollows. Picture yourself pedaling this peaceful road free of commercial traffic, loose dogs, ugly billboard signs, and long mountainous climbs. Follow the footsteps of Indian hunters, Mississippi boatmen called "Kaintucks", pioneer settlers, soldiers, and ruthless outlaws. Welcome to the Natchez Trace Parkway, one of America's premier cycling roads.

The Natchez Trace Parkway, administered by the National Park Service, follows a historic route for nearly 500 miles through Mississippi, Alabama, and Tennessee while passing remnants of a fascinating history ranging from Indian mounds to Civil War battlegrounds. The Trace also lets you experience the true South—the people and the country. Many quaint towns and three exciting cities lie off the Trace. In between are miles of peaceful countryside varying from cypress-tupelo swamps abounding with Spanish moss to rugged hillside forests of hardwoods and conifers. The woods often give way to pastoral views of bucolic pastures and fields of corn and cotton.

I hope this book will allow cyclists to truly experience the Trace in addition to providing a resource for planning their trip. Campgrounds, motels, bed and breakfasts, and food services are frequent enough to allow a comfortable journey on the entire Parkway.

Several loop tours ranging from a few hours to several days are also included. If self-contained touring isn't for you, simply travel the Parkway in the comfort of your car while taking time for any of the loop rides included in this book. These routes combine the Parkway with low volume roads that take you to interesting out-of-the-way places. While there is much gratification in pedaling the length of the Natchez Trace entirely self-contained, the loop rides offer beautiful scenery and friendly towns not found on the Parkway. Which is better? I can't say, but whatever you choose, I'm convinced that the best way to experience the Natchez Trace Parkway and the miles of nearby rural roads is on a bicycle!

THE NATURAL SETTING

The Woods

From animal path to Indian trail to wilderness road, the Natchez Trace once traversed miles and miles of unbroken virgin forests. Before the white settlers began clearing the forests, it was said that a squirrel could travel from the east coast to the Mississippi River without touching the forest floor. Over 100 species of trees and many more plants and shrubs are native to this corridor. Elevation differences along the Trace are relatively minimal, varying from 60 feet near Natchez to 1,000 feet in Tennessee, but the route covers nearly 5 degrees of latitude. Cyclists will pedal across three vegetation zones as they travel this 450-mile parkway.

Between Natchez and Jackson, the mild winters allow several subtropical trees and plants to survive. This is the Deep South where huge live oaks, magnolias, and other characteristic species thrive. The most striking distinction of this area, and a favorite of every visitor, is the Spanish moss hanging from the tree branches.

From Jackson to Tupelo, the Trace travels through mixed pine and hardwood forests. While many hardwoods found throughout the East also grow here, the Southern Yellow Pine and Loblolly Pine thrive in this climate.

North of Tupelo, the Trace enters the largest forest zone in the US, the mixed deciduous forest which includes maple, oak, hickory, beech, and poplar—just to name a few. Many of these trees display brilliant autumn foliage, and others such as the dogwood and redbud have beautiful blossoms in the spring.

In the last two hundred years, almost all of the virgin forests were cut to make way for agriculture. Nevertheless, large and small tracts of forests, usually second growth, have always dotted the landscape since European settlement. In Alabama and Mississippi, cotton quickly became king in the rich bottomlands. But eventually the Civil War, soil erosion, and the boll weevil ended its reign, and the grazing of livestock became all the depleted soil could handle. Many abandoned areas reverted to forests.

In more recent times, timber has taken the throne as the chief agricultural operation. Thousands of acres of forest near the Parkway have been logged and replaced with fast growing pine plantations. Mississippi has the dubious distinction of being the only state in the nation with a net loss of forest each year! Fortunately, the timber operations are not usually visible from the Parkway, and travelers witness long stretches of

Spanish moss along the Parkway near Port Gibson

forests interspersed with pastures and cotton fields.

In Tennessee, the Trace traverses miles of woodlands occasionally alternating with pastures and corn fields. In southern Tennessee and northern Alabama, large paper corporations such as Champion Paper and American Packaging own much of the land.

Flowering shrubs and wildflowers are seen along the Parkway from March until October. Although spring is the best time to view the flowers, several species bloom in the summer or autumn. Unfortunately, several exotic (non-native) plant species have invaded all three zones— the most notable being kudzu, known as "the vine that ate the South." Introduced from Asia as a means of erosion control, this nasty vine can engulf fields, large trees, and buildings!

Even as subdivisions spread into rural areas and forests are cut, most of the landscape you'll see while cycling the Parkway has changed little in the past 100 years. The preserved segments of the Old Trace and the many nature trails give visitors an even better semblance of the Natchez Trace of a bygone era.

The Critters

In the late 1700s, the Southeastern forests were abundant with wildlife. It was probably bison and other large animals that originally pounded the Natchez Trace into existence. The bison have vanished from this region, as have the elk, wolves, cougars, black bears, passenger pigeons, Carolina parakeets, and ivory-billed woodpeckers.

Other animals such as deer, raccoons, opossums, armadillos, woodchucks, beavers, fox, bobcats, squirrels, rabbits, vultures, eagles, hawks, quail, and many varieties of songbirds have survived if not thrived in the mix of agricultural and forested land. The alligator has escaped extinction and is found, although not common, as far north as the Jackson vicinity. The western coyote has recently invaded the Southeast, filling the predatory void left by the wolves and cougars.

The quiet ride, slow pace, and unobstructed views enjoyed by cyclists provide an excellent means to observe wildlife. Ann and I have witnessed many of these animals along the Parkway, and hopefully you will too.

The Geology
There is no better way to appreciate the geology of this region than on a bicycle—you experience every hill! In addition to your legs, your eyes will notice these subtle but distinct geological changes as you pedal the length of the Parkway.

Heading south to north, the Trace begins in the Loess Hills, a low chain of hills (up to 600 feet in elevation) that runs along the east bank of the Mississippi River from Baton Rouge to just south of Memphis. This highly erodable soil blew from the plains during a nearly continuous dust storm in the last Ice Age. The warm updrafts from the river caused the dust to settle, forming these unique hills.

Near Jeff Busby, the Trace winds through the Red Clay Hills, a series of sandstone and shale ridges known as the Wilcox Series. These relatively gentle hills (although you may not think so if you're on a loaded bike) vary from 300 to 600 feet in elevation.

Near Tupelo the Trace drops into the Tombigbee Prairie which is around 300 feet in elevation. Originally, this region consisted of grasslands, marshes, swamps, and bottomland forests, but it was later drained to make way for cotton.

North of the Tombigbee Waterway, the *real* hills begin as the Trace climbs into the Appalachian Mountains. To be truthful, these mountains are merely the Northeast Hills of Mississippi and the Freedom Hills of Alabama. Geologically speaking, these hills are the last gasp of the Cumberland Plateau, the largest wooded plateau in North America. Forming the western ridge of the Appalachians, this plateau reaches through Kentucky, Tennessee, Alabama, and Mississippi. Sandstone rock formations, characteristic of eastern Tennessee and Kentucky, are visible along the Parkway, and Tishomingo State Park contains a surprising number of large boulders forming intricate rock gardens. While the plateau reaches 3,000 feet in East Tennessee, the Northeast Hills rise to only 1,000 feet, and the Parkway itself doesn't climb above 600 feet.

After crossing the Tennessee River, the Trace begins a long climb up to the Highland Rim where it stays between 800 and 1,000 feet for 40 miles. It then drops down to the Buffalo and Duck Rivers (and a few of their tributaries) only to climb again. Numerous cascading creeks have formed a maze of narrow shady hollows cutting deep into the limestone rock of the Highland Rim.

After crossing the Tennessee Valley Divide, the Trace drops into the Central Basin. Elevations range from 400 feet near the Cumberland River where it flows though Nashville to over 1,000 feet on top of many of the knobby hills.

Parkway winding through the Freedom Hills of Alabama

THE EVOLUTION OF THE TRACE

Although I set out to write a bicycle guide, it became obvious that the Trace is much more than a scenic road and great bicycle route. The story of the Trace gives us insights into the Old Southwest and how this country, for better or worst, came to be what it is today. Hopefully as a bicycle guide author-turned-historian, I can share what I have learned of the romance and bravery along with the injustice and violence that took place along this peaceful road on which we ride.

The Prehistoric People

Animals, like humans, seek the easiest route between two points. Thousands of years ago, numerous game trails were beaten down by the hooves of buffalo and other large animals as they sought the lowest route over the ridges and hills while, at the same time, avoiding deep rivers and swamps. The earliest Americans, descendants of the Mongoloids who crossed the Bering Strait 40,000 years ago, walked these animal paths in pursuit of the large game animals during the last Ice Age. Spearpoints from these nomadic hunters of the Paleo culture have been found in all three states along the Trace.

By 8,000 B.C., the nomadic ways were gradually replaced by a slightly more settled life. The people of the Archaic culture returned to their village sites for several weeks or months each year. A small amount of food was grown to supplement their carnivorous diet. The *atlatl*, a curved wooden piece attached to the hand-held end of a spear, greatly improved the hunting ability of these people.

Around 1,000 B.C., the Woodland culture emerged as farming became more important. Pottery was utilized, and the bow and arrow replaced the *atlatl*. The Woodland culture established the custom of constructing earthen mounds to bury their dead.

The most sophisticated prehistoric Indians, known as the Mississippian culture, became prominent in the Southeast around 700 A.D. Their mounds, which often had flat tops, were much larger than the modest earthen mounds of the Woodland period. Elaborate complexes of burial and ceremonial mounds were common. The chief and his leaders probably resided on top of the mounds that also served as the center of tribal life. Art grew in importance as artisans created wood carvings, pottery and other items with purposes other than strictly utilitarian. This largely agricultural society had various divisions of labor, and social classes probably existed as well.

The series of game trails, predecessors to the Natchez Trace, had now become a major overland trade route spanning from the Gulf Coast to the Great Lakes. At the Bynum Mounds along the Parkway in Central Mississippi, archaeologists unearthed copper from the Great Lakes, flint from Ohio, green stone from East Tennessee, and shells from the Gulf of

Emerald Mound near Natchez
Courtesy of National Park Service, Natchez Trace Parkway

Mexico. Coinciding with the first European contact in the 1500s, the Mississippian culture declined and was replaced or assimilated by the more simplistic lifestyles of the Historic Tribes.

Remnants of the Woodland and Mississippian mounds can be seen at seven preserved sites along the Parkway. Near these locations, archaeologists have unearthed many artifacts that are preserved at the Parkway Visitor Center in Tupelo, local museums, and the Smithsonian Institute in Washington.

The Historic Tribes

When the Europeans first arrived, the Natchez Trace traversed lands claimed primarily by the Natchez, Choctaws, Chickasaws, and Cherokees. The small Natchez Tribe was the last culture north of Mexico to maintain the mound building ways of the Mississippian people. This highly developed society had distinct social classes, elaborate religious practices, and skilled artisans. (See p. 44 for more about the Natchez people.)

In central Mississippi, Indian legends tell of how two brothers, Shataw and Chickasaw, led their people from the West to the Hills of Origin (Nanih Waiya) now known as the Red Clay Hills. At this location, they departed, creating the Chickasaw Tribe to the north and the Choctaw Tribe to the south. Although closely related, these tribes maintained an enmity toward each other unsurpassed in Native America.

The Choctaws lived a relatively peaceful agricultural life. They were the only Southeastern tribe in which men grew their hair long. They also practiced the unique custom of flattening their infants' heads; hence the French dubbed them "Flatheads." Unlike their brethren, the smaller Chickasaw Tribe primarily hunted and was reputed to be the fiercest warriors of the Southeast.

The Cherokees never resided near the Natchez Trace although they claimed the northern portion of this future pioneer road. Instead the largest tribe in the Southeast dwelled in the Appalachian Mountains and valleys of East Tennessee, Georgia, and North Carolina. Hunting parties frequently toured the Tennessee and Alabama portions of the Trace in hopes of returning to their villages with meats and hides.

The Explorers

In 1539, Spanish explorer Hernando de Soto landed in Florida with 1,000 men and began a perilous 3-year overland journey. Searching for riches of a non-existent empire (De Soto gained great wealth in his previous conquests in South America), he led his men across ten Southeastern states. The expedition spent the winter among the Chickasaw Indians until they were attacked in March of 1541. This may not have come as a surprise since these *conquistadors* had ransacked Indian villages and captured Chief Tuscaloosa of the Choctaw Tribe. The De Soto Expedition fled westward, crossing the Natchez Trace, and became the first known Europeans to lay eyes on the Mississippi River. De Soto died of fever in 1542, and his weighted body was put to rest in the Mississippi River near Natchez.

After De Soto's visit, the valleys of the Mississippi basin would not see another white man for 130 years. The French came next when Marquette and Joliett explored the Mississippi River as far south as Greenville, Mississippi in 1673. Nine years later Robert Cavelier sieur de las Salle explored the great river all the way to its mouth, claiming this vast untamed region for France. La Salle stopped at the high bluffs of Natchez and visited a Natchez village (probably Emerald Mound) describing it as a place of "beautiful eminence."

A Tale of Two Settlements

By 1713, the French established a trading post near the Grand Village of the Natchez Nation and three years later constructed Fort Rosalie on a high bluff above the Mississippi River in present day Natchez. Upon hearing that the French were planning to acquire their tribal lands, the small Natchez

Tribe fooled the French into believing the Choctaws were going to attack their settlement. After being armed and trusted by the French, the Natchez rebelled in 1729 and attacked the isolated fort, killing 250 men and taking 300 women and children as prisoners. The victory for the Natchez people was short-lived, for the French struck back and annihilated the last tribe of the mound culture north of Mexico. While a few members fled to be assimilated by neighboring tribes, the Natchez Indians were among the earliest to be decimated by European encroachment.

Intent on establishing their superiority after the Fort Rosalie Massacre, the French headed north in 1736 with their Choctaw allies to subdue the Chickasaws who were friendly with the British. The fierce Chickasaw warriors soundly defeated the French in the Battle of Ackia near present-day Tupelo. France never regained the upper hand in this region, and, following the French and Indian War in 1762, relinquished her land east of the Mississippi to Great Britain.

The British immediately set out to create a new colony of British West Florida and rebuilt Fort Rosalie, changing its name to Fort Panmure. With the Natchez Tribe now extinct, the mild climate and fertile land became attractive to settlers from the Northeast. During the American Revolution, several British sympathizers moved to Natchez only to find Spain grabbing control of the territory while the British were pre-occupied with fighting the colonists. Spain exerted little influence over the Natchez Territory, and the Anglo-Americans continued to establish plantations in the countryside.

Meanwhile in Middle Tennessee, the "long hunters" had crossed the Appalachians to hunt and trap in the unsettled wilderness of the Cumberland Valley. In 1779-80 James Robertson, leading a group of settlers overland, and John Donelson, traveling by flatboat via the Tennessee, Ohio, and Cumberland Rivers, established a settlement named Fort Nashborough (renamed Nashville in 1784) along a bend in the Cumberland River.

In the next few years, additional settlements and forts were built in the region. From 1781-1792, these wilderness outposts suffered numerous attacks by the Cherokees including a well-planned attack on Fort Nashborough in 1781. The Indians lured the men out of the fort and then began an ambush. Mrs. Robertson may have averted a massacre by releasing the dogs who, snarling and growling, frightened the Indians and allowed the men to retreat into the fort. As the Indian hostilities subsided in the 1790s, agriculture prospered, and increasing numbers of settlers, many with Revolutionary War land grants, began clearing the forests in north central Tennessee.

The Boatmen's Trail

In the 1780s, settlements of the Tennessee and Ohio Valley had grown sufficiently to require a practical means of selling farm produce to larger markets. Shipping overland to the East Coast was nearly impossible due to the lack of decent roads and the amount of labor required to haul the goods. On the other hand, to get the goods to Natchez or New Orleans, all one had to do was build a flatboat and float down the inland waterways using a combination of the Cumberland, Ohio, and the Mississippi Rivers. There was only one problem—the boats couldn't get back up the river easily. So for the next two to four weeks, these brave farmers-turned-boatmen would embark by foot or horseback on the difficult and perilous overland journey home.

And so the "Boatmen's Era" began. By 1790, 64 boatloads of produce were delivered to the markets in Natchez where they were exported to the East Coast and Europe. In the ensuing years, thousands of Kaintucks, as they were called regardless of where they came from, arrived in Natchez and New Orleans to sell farm produce, home industry products, and even the timbers from their boats.

The overland journey began at Natchez-Under-the-Hill, a place described by one Southern writer as "a hell-raising,

Drawing of flatboat

rampaging sin-spot, Mecca of men who wanted liquor, song, and women." In the mud of the river's edge, an assortment of disreputable establishments sprung up, all with one objective—to tempt the gullible Kaintucks into losing their hard-earned money. Gambling dens, dance halls, bar rooms, and boarding houses offered an unusual taste of civilization on the western frontier. It is said that many boatmen left Natchez with little more to show for a year's labor than the clothes they were wearing!

Once beyond the temptations of Natchez-Under-the-Hill, the 450-mile trek enjoyed by cyclists today, was a dreaded ordeal for the Kaintucks traveling by horse or foot. In the 1790s, the Natchez Trace was still a narrow trail through Indian Territory, and travelers had to contend with poisonous snakes, hordes of mosquitoes, unfriendly Indians, swollen rivers, and deep mud that often halted progress for days at a time. With no accommodations beyond Bayou Pierre (50 miles out of Natchez), most nights were spent on the forest floor whether it be during a chilling rain storm or a hot sultry night teaming with insects.

As if this weren't enough, the Kaintucks dreaded the bandits most of all. Traveling with their newly acquired money on an isolated wilderness road, they were perfect prey for highwaymen. The most feared outlaws were the Harpe Brothers who terrorized travelers and settlers from Natchez to Kentucky. Big and Little Harpe were known for particularly grisly murders including that of Big Harpe's *own* child. Another story of their misdeeds occurred at the King's Tavern in Natchez, now a restaurant. A woman was visiting the post office at the tavern with her young child who began crying. Big Harpe rushed in, took the child by the ankles, and slammed it against the wall killing the innocent child. (Mysteriously in recent times, people have heard a baby crying in the tavern when no young children were present.) Big Harpe was killed and beheaded in 1799 in Kentucky by a man who had lost his wife and child to Big Harpe's murderous ways. Little Harpe met his fate in 1803 and was hanged along the Trace just north of Natchez. Even without the Harpe Brothers, bands of criminals such as the Mason Gang flourished along the Trace well into the 19th Century.

Drawing of Kaintucks traveling the Trace
Courtesy of National Park Service, Natchez Trace Parkway

The Wilderness Journey Improves

As traffic increased, so did the amenities. The Kaintucks often stopped at isolated pioneer cabins in hopes of a meal and a place to sleep. Soon many such places became inns (often referred to as stands) where travelers could spend the night in basic comfort before continuing their journey in the morning. By 1810, over 50 stands were operating along the Trace, each a day's journey apart. Many of the stands in Indian Territory were run by Indians, half-breeds, or those married to Indians. Chief George Colbert, a half-Scot half-Chickasaw, greatly improved travel (and his pocket book!) by opening a ferry across the Tennessee River in 1800 and shared profits from the Duck River ferry that opened in 1803.

After Mississippi became a U.S. territory in 1798, improved communications were needed between Natchez and the rest of the country. President Jefferson decided that "a road from Nashville to Natchez was necessary for the safety and welfare of the nation." That same year, treaties were negotiated with the Choctaw and Chickasaw Tribes allowing the U.S. army to improve the Trace and establish it as a post road. After widening over 250 miles of the roadway, bridging numerous creeks and constructing causeways in low-lying areas, the army abandoned the project in 1803. Although the route had been greatly improved, building a road through miles of wilderness was more difficult than anyone had imagined.

The postal route opened in 1801 with post riders reaching Natchez in as little as ten days. Leaving Nashville at 8:00 p.m. with the mail, government dispatches, a few newspapers, along with a blanket and a half bushel of corn for themselves, the post riders often rode well after dark. Five days later, they would exchange horses at the post office at Tockshish before continuing on to Natchez.

Famous Travelers

Several well-known names are inextricably tied to the Natchez Trace, the most notable being Andrew Jackson. Prior to his presidency, the hot-tempered lawyer from Nashville traveled the Trace many times including trips to negotiate treaties with the Indians, to marry Rachel Robards at the Springfield Plantation near Natchez, and to lead his troops home from New Orleans after defeating the British in the War of 1812.

Another hero's life ended tragically while traveling the Trace in Tennessee. On one autumn night in 1809, a gun shot sounded at the isolated Grinder's Stand, and Meriwether Lewis, former leader of the Lewis and Clark expedition and Governor of the Louisiana Territory, lay dead in his room. Was it murder or suicide? The mystery will always linger.

Men and women used the Trace for a variety of reasons, but few made this dangerous journey in search of birds. Renowned ornithologist John James Audobon did just that and also taught at the Elizabeth Female Academy in Washington, Mississippi.

Along with the heroes, numerous fugitives also used the Trace. Aaron Burr, the former Vice President under Thomas Jefferson, hid from the law in Tennessee, Alabama, and Mississippi. Accused of conspiring with Spain to annex the western U.S., Burr, who had earlier killed Alexander Hamilton in a duel, was apprehended twice in Mississippi but acquitted each time.

The Decline of the Trace

The steamboat *New Orleans* sailing its maiden voyage from Pittsburgh to New Orleans in 1811 heralded the beginning of the end of the Natchez Trace. Within a few years, travelers could travel upriver on loud, smoky steamboats traveling at a "brisk" 3 miles per hour—pure luxury compared to perils and hardships of the Trace. Not surprisingly, the use of the Natchez Trace quickly declined. Furthering its demise, the government began construction of the Jackson Military Road to the east which reduced the trip between Nashville and New Orleans by 200 miles. In the 1820s, this new road with its 35-foot wide roadbed must have seemed like a major interstate compared to the rutted path of the Natchez Trace. Over the years, the Trace faded away as the forest reclaimed the road that had opened the wilderness. In some areas, portions of this historic road were utilized as a local road connecting the growing communities. Nevertheless, after years of foot, horse, and wagon traffic, sunken remnants of the original Trace can still be seen along the Parkway nearly 180 years after its decline.

The Trail of Tears

Along with the Trace, the proud Native Americans of the old Southwest would soon become part of the past—victims of America's hunger for land. When Mississippi was admitted to the Union in 1817, over half the state was part of Indian Territory. In the Treaty at Doak's Stand (1820), the Choctaw agreed to cede five million acres or one-third of their land after Andrew Jackson threatened them with extinction. But five million acres were not enough, and ten years later the Mississippi Legislature denied all rights to Native Americans living within the state. That same year the Treaty of Dancing Rabbit Creek sent the Choctaws, many of who had become farmers and Christians, from their homelands forever. Two years later, the Chickasaw signed the Treaty of Pontitock, and the entire region was open for settlement. During the 1830s, the Choctaw, Chickasaw, Cherokee, Creek, and Seminole Tribes began a long arduous journey to Oklahoma, a journey now known as the Trail of Tears. During this shameful episode in U.S. history, countless numbers of Indians perished before reaching their new home.

The Plantation Era

The beginning of the Boatmen's Era in the 1780s interestingly coincides with the dawning of the plantation economy. While the Kaintucks were trudging north on the Natchez Trace, the nearby fields south of Indian Territory were being cleared for cotton. After Indian removal, the cotton kingdom spread north to the Tennessee River in Alabama. Although some cotton was grown on the Highland Rim in Tennessee, the soil here was better suited for livestock, corn, and tobacco.

In the early 1800s, a fortunate few found they could make an unprecedented amount of money with fertile land, cotton seeds, and the all-important slave labor. The backbreaking toil and long hours of uncompensated servitude of the African-American slaves enabled the plantation economy to thrive. Numerous wagons bringing the year's cotton harvest to market rolled along portions of the Natchez Trace.

As the center of the cotton empire, Natchez became the wealthiest city in the nation with more millionaires than any other city. Wealthy planters built lavish homes in Natchez in addition to their magnificent plantation homes in Mississippi and Louisiana. A few planters owned more than one cotton plantation, and they often spent their summers in the cooler Northeast. Men from all over the U.S. came to Natchez to make their fortunes in cotton, but more than a few lost everything in this prosperous town.

The Civil War

In the spring of 1861, Mississippi, Alabama, and Tennessee seceded from the Union along with eight other Southern states. By this time, the Natchez Trace was no longer a major road; however, remnants of the old path bisected the heart of the western theater of the bloodiest war ever fought on U.S. soil. After the Union army occupied Nashville with minimal opposition, the first major conflict near the Natchez Trace occurred in April of 1862 at the Battle of Shiloh along the Tennessee River (50 miles west of the Natchez Trace). Here General Grant repelled a major Confederate offensive. Vicksburg, a port on the Mississippi River 50 miles west of Jackson, was an important Confederate stronghold. Until Vicksburg fell, the Union would never gain full control of the river which was crucial to isolate the interior region of the South. General Grant, being unable to take Vicksburg, marched his troops south along the west side of the Mississippi and attempted to cross at the town of Grand Gulf. After being repulsed again, Grant continued down river to Bruinsburg just north of Natchez and entered the state of Mississippi unopposed.

With only minor skirmishes, the Union troops marched north on the Natchez Trace from Port Gibson to Jackson, capturing the capital in May of 1863. Grant turned his forces west and attempted to take Vicksburg from the east, thus avoiding the fortifications along the river. Once again, the Union forces could not break Vicksburg's defenses, so Grant surrounded the city and held it under siege for nearly three weeks of constant bombardment. On July 4, 1862, Vicksburg surrendered, and the Union soon controlled the mighty Mississippi River.

With the western campaign nearly finished, General Grant was promoted to supreme commander of the Union Army, and General William T. Sherman took command of the western armies with the objective of marching from Nashville to Atlanta and then on to Savannah, Georgia. In the summer of 1864, Confederate General Nathan Bedford Forrest was given the task of cutting Sherman's supply lines. General Sherman, realizing that the single track railroad from Nashville to Chattanooga was vulnerable, ordered General Sturgis out of Memphis to subdue Forrest's army encamped near Tupelo. They met at Brices Cross Roads, 15 miles north of Tupelo where Forrest with 3,500 troops soundly defeated the 8,000-man army of General Sturgis.

One month later, 14,000 Union forces marched south to Tupelo to, as Sherman ordered, "Go out and follow Forrest to the death, if it cost 10,000 lives and breaks the Treasury." For two days, the Confederates attacked the Union lines near Tupelo but were repeatedly repulsed and suffered heavy casualties. Low on food and ammunition, the Union army was not faring very well either in the July heat and finally withdrew. In November and December of 1864, the Confederate army made one last futile attempt to halt Sherman's "March to the Sea" by attacking his supply lines in Nashville and Franklin, Tennessee.

The Modern-Day Parkway

After the war the economy collapsed, and countless buildings, roads, and farms had been destroyed. Although the people did their best to rebuild, much of the rural South remained impoverished from the Civil War to the Great Depression of the 1930s.

In 1905, an article by John Swain appeared in *Everybody's Magazine* about the history and romance of Natchez Trace. Within a few years, the Daughters of the American Revolution began erecting markers along the route of the Natchez Trace in all three states, and interest in this forgotten road grew.

With rural Mississippi being hard hit by the Great Depression, Mississippi Congressman Jeff Busby introduced legislation calling for the National Park Service to survey the "Old Indian Trail known as the Natchez Trace, with a view of constructing a national road on the route to be known as the Natchez Trace Parkway." So in 1937 a public works project of the New Deal came to the rural South, and construction of the Parkway began. It wasn't until 68 years later, in May of 2005, that the final two segments near Jackson and Natchez were completed. Just like the Kaintucks who trudged along the Trace 200 years ago, you can now travel for nearly 450 miles and never see a traffic light or a stop sign.

GENERAL INFORMATION

TERRAIN

Let us begin by dispelling this myth among cyclists planning to tour the Trace: *It is mostly downhill from Nashville to Natchez.* Wrong! While the Northern Terminus is at 700 feet in elevation and Natchez is around 200 feet, cyclists will contend with more than 10,000 feet in accumulated climbs in either direction. So what's a difference of 500 feet going to matter?

Fortunately, most bicyclists find the terrain along the Natchez Trace to be ideal—enough hills to make the ride interesting but no mountainous ascents. The land becomes increasingly hilly north of Tombigbee Waterway as the Trace winds through the Appalachian foothills of northern Mississippi and Alabama and then ascends the Highland Rim in Tennessee. Cyclists may climb up to 3,000 feet in one day, but only a few individual climbs are over 300 feet. Plenty of "payoffs" are guaranteed as the Trace drops into secluded hollows. The section between the Old Trace Drive and the Water Valley Overlook (mp 376-412) is probably the toughest with approximately 1,800 feet of climbing in either direction in less than 40 miles. Cyclists should be grateful that the Parkway is well-graded. Looking at the surrounding terrain, it is easy to imagine the original travelers contending with these steep hills.

PARKWAY EMERGENCY
call
1-800-300-PARK
(7275)

South of Tupelo the Parkway becomes more level, but numerous gentle hills will constantly keep you shifting. Near Witch Dance (mp 233) and Jeff Busby (mp 193) a few 200-foot climbs will convince you that central Mississippi is *not* entirely flat. The most level terrain occurs near Jackson and extends down to Port Gibson. Southbound cyclists will find that the Trace delivers its final punch as they enter the Loess Hills near Natchez. While none of the climbs are extremely difficult, there are plenty of them.

CYCLING THE SEASONS OF THE SOUTH

The Natchez Trace offers year round cycling opportunities, but you must plan properly. While the South is infamous for sweltering summer conditions, occasional Arctic coldfronts can penetrate this region in the winter. Rain is possible anytime of year, and the wind (I'm sorry to say) can come from any direction. While summertime weather is usually predictable (hot and humid!), weather patterns from late fall to early spring are often wacky. This is caused by alternating weather influences from the warm Gulf and Arctic coldfronts. The average summer temperature in Natchez is only one or two degrees higher than Nashville, but winter temperatures average about 15 degrees warmer.

Autumn—Local cyclists rejoice in mid-September when the first coldfront comes down from the north. The winds pick up, the heat and humidity drop, and the skies become a deep blue. The days may still be in the 80s, but the nights are pleasantly cool. Although the heat and humidity may return, it will be only for a brief time, and great cycling weather is just around the corner. By October the weather is usually ideal with 70s for highs. On the northern half of the Trace, lows occasionally dip below freezing near the end of the month. This is the driest time of year, but slow moving fronts may bring rain for several days. In November, the weather on the northern portion of the Trace becomes chilly but still enjoyable, and pleasant 60-degree weather often prevails down south.

For autumn cycling, you'll need to bring a variety of clothing that can easily be layered according to the changing conditions. Later in the season, hope for an idyllic Indian summer but be prepared for winter-like weather.

Bicycling is an excellent way to view the fall color along the Trace. In Tennessee and Alabama, leaf color will start to appear by mid-October and peak by late October or early November. Although not as brilliant as the northern Trace, the mixed pine and hardwood forests south of Tupelo display a pleasing variety of reds and yellows in mid-November.

Spring—As the dogwoods are blooming and the streams are flowing at their fullest, spring is a wonderful time to bike the Natchez Trace. Ann and I have fond memories of March and April bike rides through miles of flowering dogwood and redbuds that border the Parkway. We also recall the "1993 Spring Thaw Ride" we led for the Nashville Bicycle Club in March. It snowed the night before, and a bitter wind was blowing snow everywhere that morning. For some reason, no one else showed up for that ride!

March is normally the wettest month on the Trace, so you may get a good soaking in between those lovely spring days. By May, the large weather systems are replaced by brief thunderstorms that may bring very violent weather. Look for shelter and stay off your bike if lightning is likely (your tires will not protect you!). As summer approaches, so does the heat and humidity, but we usually find rides that end by noon to be enjoyable well into June. Like autumn, a good layering system is best to deal with the variety of weather Mother Nature may deliver in March and April. Full rain gear is highly recommended!

Summer—We don't understand why they call these the "dog days of summer." It is difficult to find a dog in the South with the energy to chase a cyclist on a stifling July afternoon. We've all heard the saying "It's not the heat, it's the humidity." When they both climb above 90, you'll find it is the heat *and* the humidity! By mid-summer, we long for a breeze, even a headwind, to bring down the oppressive humidity. Thunderstorms may occur, but leave your rain gear at home and enjoy the cool shower. Only the most heat tolerant cyclists should attempt to tour the Trace in the middle of summer. If you are camping, expect muggy and possibly buggy conditions at the campgrounds. Forget the sleeping bag—a sheet packed in a plastic trash bag will be sufficient.

Day rides, on the other hand, can be enjoyable if they are well planned. Here are some tips:

- *The earlier you start the better.* If you are on the bike a half hour before sunrise you will have reasonable temperatures and are likely to enjoy a lovely misty daybreak. Plan on finishing your ride by 10 or 11 a.m. before the mercury starts climbing fast.

- *Don't ride hard but keep moving.* In hot weather, your body requires more energy to cool itself which means less energy for pedaling. Bike at a relaxed pace while spinning at a fairly fast cadence (80-100 rpm) especially when climbing. On the other hand if you stop, the lack of wind blowing against your skin will prevent the perspiration from evaporating, so keep moving unless you are really tired.

- *Drink, drink, drink.* Drink before you ride *and* drink before you're thirsty. Carry at least two large water bottles if you will be riding more than 15 miles with no water stops. Drinking an electrolyte drink (Gatorade, etc.) will help keep your energy level up and may prevent muscle cramps. The country stores near the Parkway sell such drinks (and they are cold!). Drinking too much of certain sports drinks sometimes causes nausea, so I suggest carrying both water *and* an electrolyte drink. If you are perspiring profusely, feel exhausted, and look pale, you may have heat exhaustion and should immediately rest in the shade while drinking plenty of fluids.

- *Plan your rest stops.* Take breaks at a market, restaurant, or visitor center where you can relax in an air conditioned environment. (My wife can often be seen sticking her head in the freezer of some little grocery on a hot day!) If a climate-controlled break is not possible, look for a shady area that is open to the breezes (if there are any).
- *Use sunscreen.* Although you should use it year round, be especially conscious about applying sunscreen during the summer. Besides endangering your skin, sunburn can drain your energy by requiring more blood to nourish the skin cells. We find that the sweat-proof sunscreens such as the sport lotion made by Coppertone work well in hot, humid conditions.
- *In the land of cotton—don't wear it.* A light-colored jersey made out of synthetic material such as Coolmax allows perspiration to evaporate and does not cling to the skin like cotton when wet. A well-ventilated helmet keeps air flowing across the scalp.

Winter—South of Jackson, the Natchez Trace offers fairly reliable winter cycling with temperatures averaging in the upper 50s. Although the temperatures north of Jackson are usually chilly, cycling is still enjoyable with proper clothing. While rain is more common, frozen precipitation may occur anywhere along the Trace although it is more common on the northern half.

Beware of sudden changes in weather. On several occasions in Nashville, we have experienced highs near 60 degrees, only to find that the next day's temperature dips into the teens. While brisk sunny days are common, cold rainy days and sub-freezing cold snaps make extended touring very risky (although some have done it). Should you opt to do this, bring winter clothing including a winter sleeping bag if camping, and be flexible with layover days. Check the long-range weather forecast to determine if your tour is feasible. Day rides, on the other hand, can be enjoyable anywhere along the Trace during the winter as long as you avoid the bad weather days.

Proper clothing is always essential, because even 60 degrees can seem cold when you add a 15 mph wind-chill factor. On the other hand, exercise generates body heat, so it will take some practice to find the right combination of clothing. Pay particular attention to your head, neck, hands, and feet because these areas are especially vulnerable to the cold. Materials such as polypropylene, capilene, and wool will keep you much warmer and drier than cotton. We recommend wearing a windproof shell that you can easily unzip when you climb a hill and zip up again for the chilly descent. Remember that like hot weather, cold weather also saps your energy.

Nashville Average Temperature (F) and Precipitation (inches)

	High	Low	Precip.		High	Low	Precip.
Jan	46	28	4.5	July	90	69	3.8
Feb	51	30	4.0	Aug	89	68	3.4
Mar	60	38	5.6	Sept	83	61	3.7
Apr	71	48	4.5	Oct	72	48	2.6
May	79	57	4.6	Nov	59	38	3.5
June	87	65	3.7	Dec	50	31	4.6

Jackson Average Temperature (F) and Precipitation (inches)

	High	Low	Precip.		High	Low	Precip.
Jan	58	36	4.5	July	93	71	4.38
Feb	62	38	4.6	Aug	93	70	3.6
Mar	69	43	5.6	Sept	88	64	3.0
Apr	78	53	4.7	Oct	80	52	2.2
May	85	60	4.4	Nov	69	42	3.9
June	91	68	3.4	Dec	61	37	5.0

Unusual March weather near Nashville

ROAD CONDITIONS

The Trace offers an ideal cycling environment with light traffic, adequate visibility, and no commercial traffic (which means no big trucks!). The low number of intersections also makes the Parkway safer than most urban or rural roads. The roadway consists of a 12-foot lane in each direction with no paved shoulders. Although some cyclists prefer more room, many riders appreciate the aesthetic of a winding country lane. There is almost always a level grassy area adjacent to the road in case of emergencies.

While much of the Natchez Trace sees less than 2,000 motorists per day, the volume of traffic is substantially higher just north of Jackson and near Tupelo due to commuters using the Parkway. Nearly 8,000 motorists use the Parkway daily near these cities. Although the local drivers are accustomed to seeing cyclists, you may want to avoid commuting hours if possible. The Park Service encourages cyclists to use the sections south of Jackson and north of Cherokee, Alabama.

Recently, the Park Service has employed a resurfacing method known as chip seal where the worn roadway is sprayed with a thin layer of asphalt topped by a layer of finely crushed limestone aggregate. Although the Park Service claims to save 80% of normal resurfacing costs with this method, some cyclists feel it is at the expense of their hands and tush. While I don't consider chip seal to be too rough, it definitely is not the smooth asphalt that cyclists love. For a more comfortable ride, try the following:

- Use padded bike shorts, a cushioned saddle, padded gloves, and cushioned handlebar tape. When combined, these items greatly reduce the vibrations caused by the roadway.
- Bike where the right tire track of auto traffic has worn the crushed rock. The pavement is considerably smoother here than near the edge of the roadway.
- If the road surface is still bothersome, keep your tires inflated at 10-15 psi below their maximum.

SAFETY AND REGULATIONS

The Natchez Trace Parkway is designated as a national bike route, and cyclists are welcomed to use the Parkway. Park rangers do enforce all traffic regulations regarding bicycling including the following:

- Bicycle riders must comply with all applicable traffic regulations. Bicycle riders shall keep well to the side of the road and shall keep the cycle under complete control at all times. Bicycles shall not be ridden abreast of one another except on roads designed for cycle use only. (*You are permitted to pass other cyclists.*)
- Each bicycle must exhibit a white light or reflector on the front and a red light or reflector on the rear during periods of low visibility or during the period between sundown and sunup.
- Bicyclists shall ride in groups of six or less, keeping at least 300 feet between groups.

Using common sense is the best way to have a safe and enjoyable trip on the Parkway. The most obvious precaution is to wear a helmet. Wearing bright colors (such as orange, yellow, or red) will make you much more visible to motorists. Experienced cyclists generally ride along the line of the right tire track, about 2-3 feet from the edge of the roadway. This requires motorists to cross the center line when passing and discourages drivers from attempting to pass when oncoming traffic is approaching or visibility is not adequate. While this may seem risky to some, the chances of being hit from behind are much less than being squeezed off the edge of the road-way. Keeping 2-3 feet from the edge (more is needed on fast descents) also allows room to spare in case of road hazards or wind gusts. If a motorist is unable to pass after a few minutes, do them a favor by pulling off the roadway when safe to let him or her pass.

Most cycling accidents do not involve motor vehicles, so be alert and make sure your bike is in good condition. Check that the brakes are properly working, the tires are correctly inflated, and everything (including rack bolts, straps, etc.) is secure.

PARKING

The rangers ask that you do not leave your car parked overnight along the Parkway. (Cars left more than 24 hours will be considered abandoned and towed.) Overnight parking is usually available at ranger stations and maintenance yards, but you *must* call the Parkway Headquarters (see *Appendices*) to make arrangements.

Parking for day rides is allowed at the numerous interpretive stops and picnic areas along the Trace. While the rangers prefer that you utilize designated parking areas, parking is allowed on the roadway's grass shoulder provided you are completely off the pavement and the ground is not wet.

NIGHT RIDING

On several occasions, Ann and I have joined friends for summer night rides on the Parkway. The Natchez Trace takes on an entirely different aura when the moon illuminates the rural landscape with a bluish haze. The lightning bugs put on a fascinating light show while the crickets and frogs serenade throughout the night. Although you can see forever on a clear moonlit night, motorists cannot, so proper lighting is essential. For this reason, the Park Service does not encourage night riding. Using reflectors only as required invites disaster because they only work when illuminated by headlights. We each use a flashing red light in the rear and a front white light in addition to our reflective vest.

NATURAL HAZARDS

Although not the wilderness road it once was, numerous hazards (or sometimes mere nuisances) await the unwary self-propelled traveler. The number one concern is obviously weather-related conditions such as dehydration, heat stroke, and hypothermia. Of course your best defense is to be prepared and know your limitations. If dangerous conditions begin to occur, seek shelter and do not continue. Call 800/300-PARK and give the park ranger your location including nearest milepost. If a phone is not available, ask a passing motorist to call at the first opportunity.

Insects—The South has lots of them, and they're big! Biting insects are generally not a problem while you are cycling, but they may find you if you stop for very long. Even when camping in the summer, I have never encountered voracious hordes of mosquitoes, but a bug proof tent and insect repellent are certainly advisable. Beware of ticks in brushy areas or under low hanging trees; inspect yourself frequently if you go through such areas.

You may want to think twice before taking an afternoon snooze on the miles of grass along the Parkway. Nearly invisible mite larvae known as chiggers, a southern specialty, often reside in the grass. They dig into the skin causing itching and irritation, but not until they have left their helpless victim. Avoid walking in tall grass, but if you must, shoes, socks, long pants, and repellent will help you avoid this misery. Although cortisone cream helps, ChiggerX is our favorite remedy for those little buggers.

Black widow and brown recluse spiders reside along the entire Trace. Incidences of bites are quite rare, but should one occur, seek medical attention immediately. Finally, watch out for small mounds of dirt. I once had the misfortune of pulling off on the shoulder and disturbing a mound of fire ants!

Snakes—The rattlesnake, copperhead, and water moccasin (or cottonmouth) are all very poisonous snakes that reside in the South. Bites are very rare and usually pose no serious health risk if treated immediately. In the rare case of a snake bite, keep the victim (or yourself) as calm as possible while keeping the affected area below the heart. First aid such as incisions or tourniquets is not recommended, but you must seek help immediately. Staying on the road or maintained trails and keeping alert is the best way to avoid unfriendly reptilian encounters.

Plants—Poison ivy grows throughout the East including along the entire Natchez Trace. It can take the form of a vine, shrub, or ground cover. Remember the saying "Leaves of three, let it be." Wash the area of skin that may have been exposed and apply a cortisone cream should a rash develop. Besides this bothersome plant, various trees and plants have nasty thorns. The nature trails along the Parkway are generally clear of such hazards.

Natural Bandits—Although they are not the outlaws that terrorized the Kaintucks, there may be four-legged thieves who love to steal food. Raccoons, skunks, possums, rodents, dogs, and coyotes often reside near the campgrounds. If you don't have a car in which to store your food, hang your food in a stuff sack from a tree, keeping the bag at least 5 feet off the ground and a safe distance from the trunk or other branches that a raccoon might be able to climb. Check to make sure there is not an ant colony on the tree. We never keep food in our tent. Although most mammals won't enter the tent when you're in it, insects such as ants will. I have heard of fire ants chewing through the floor of a tent!

PLANNING YOUR TRIP

While some cyclists pedal the entire Parkway in four days, others take two weeks. Most riders comfortably complete the trip in 7 to10 days. Hammerhead cyclists who simply want to ride fast and hard all day love the Parkway—no stop signs and no intersections to navigate! For those who like to stop to smell the roses, numerous historic sites and nature trails beckon the cyclist to see what the Natchez Trace is all about. Also, several towns lie a short distance off the Trace, and it would be a shame not to visit these remnants of Small Town, America. The day rides in this book make wonderful excursions for those wanting to take a layover day for additional exploring.

There are no services (such as grocery stores, motels, etc.) adjacent to the roadway except for a small market at Jeff Busby. Bed and breakfasts, motels, cafes, campgrounds, and numerous small country stores are often less than a mile off the Trace, but you have to know where to find them. Hopefully with this trusty guidebook you will have everything a touring cyclist needs to know including the most important concerns—where to eat and sleep.

Lodging—The Natchez Trace provides an ideal "credit card tour," with reasonably priced motels and charming historic bed and breakfasts situated along the entire corridor. Currently, the cyclist is never more than a 60-mile ride from a comfortable bed, and 20 to 30-mile days are often possible. Although the cities have ample motel rooms, you should make reservations at all B&Bs and at motels in small towns or rural areas. Reservations are highly recommended in Natchez during the Historic Homes Pilgrimages in October,

December, and April. B&B travelers may have to spend at least one night in a no-frill motel. Likewise, those desiring lower budget accommodations may have to splurge for a reasonably priced B&B on a couple of nights.

The Natchez Trace Bed & Breakfast Service (see *Appendices*) books trips at B&Bs all along the Trace. Kay Jones, who also runs the Ridgetop B&B in Tennessee, helps cyclists with the various logistics including airport transportation and shuttles to B&Bs several miles off the Trace. The Natchez Pilgrimage Tours also makes reservations for several B&Bs in the Natchez area.

Camping—For those who like to rough it, the Natchez Trace offers a variety of camping opportunities from primitive to fully developed sites, with most campgrounds being in a wooded setting. Camping facilities are never more than 50 miles apart except near Jackson where camping is available but difficult to access due to busy roads.

The Park Service operates three campgrounds at Rocky Springs, Jeff Busby, and Meriwether Lewis. The campgrounds have running water and flush toilets but no showers. They operate on a first come, first served basis and may fill up in the Fall and Spring, so try to get there early enough to claim a spot. In addition, there are five cyclists-only campgrounds strategically located to provide a reasonable day's ride between camping locations. These camping areas have tables and nearby restrooms, but are not usually well marked, so follow the instructions closely to find them.

Although no fee is charged for any of the Parkway campgrounds, most cyclists seem to think that the occasional hot shower is a grand idea. Fortunately, several public and private campgrounds with showers are located near the Trace, but on some nights you'll probably have to do without this luxury. Please plan your overnight stays carefully because the Park Service does not permit camping except in designated campgrounds.

Dining—The South is famous for its home cookin', and numerous family-owned restaurants will allow you to sample the local cuisine. Many of these establishments are known as a "meat n' three." In other words you get to choose the main course along with three vegetables which often includes questionable vegetables such as macaroni with cheese and fried apples. Traditional southern vegetables such as turnip greens, fried okra, mashed potatoes, and black eyed peas are readily available to replenish your energy. Being vegetarians, Ann and I simply substitute an additional vegetable and enjoy a very filling meal, especially if we indulge in the scrumptious pies for which the South is famous. Keep in the mind that many eateries may be opened only for lunch or dinner and are often closed on Sunday (and sometimes on a weekday). The secret to successful bike touring is to stay flexible and always carry spare food in case none is available.

The larger towns offer a variety of unique dining opportunities ranging from ethnic fare to traditional Southern cuisine. Bike touring is more than pedaling, it's experiencing the local culture, and sampling the cuisine is a good way to start. We usually avoid fast food and chain restaurants for that very reason. This guide includes a sampling of interesting places to eat in Natchez, Port Gibson, Jackson, Kosciusko, Tupelo, Franklin, and Nashville.

Groceries—Numerous small markets lie within a mile of the Parkway, but once again you'll need to follow this guide to know where to find them. Most country stores have snacks and cold drinks including beverages such as Gatorade. Several have deli sandwiches, and a few even offer hot lunches. In a pinch, camping cyclists can usually find enough groceries to make dinner and breakfast although the selection is often limited to canned goods, pasta, rice, and cereals. For gourmet camp cuisine, I suggest you stock up at the supermarkets that are located 1-2 days apart.

Country store near the Parkway north of Rocky Springs

TRANSPORTATION LOGISTICS

For those wishing to bike the Natchez Trace one way, there are various means of getting you and your bike to wherever you need to go. I recommend that you make all necessary arrangements in advance so your bike vacation will be hassle-free.

Air Service—Nashville and Jackson are served by airports with commercial flights daily. Tupelo is served by a commuter airport, but generally commuter flights do not take boxed bicycles as luggage. The fee for bikes is usually $45 dollars each way, so you might want to consider shipping your bike in advance. Natchez does not have airport service but Baton Rouge, 110 miles south along the Adventure Cycling Great Rivers Route (see *Appendices*), has a commercial airport. The roads to the Nashville and Jackson airports are less than ideal for cycling, so you might want to have a station wagon taxi give you a lift.

Grayline Downtown Airport Express (615/275-1180) and several hotels offer convenient shuttle service to downtown Nashville, and they will take boxed bikes. Downtown Nashville, with its numerous night clubs and historic attractions, is an excellent place to begin or end your tour. Plus you can officially complete the ride from the banks of the Cumberland River to the Mississippi River (just like the boatmen did 200 years ago). The bike ride from downtown to the Trace is not too bad if you avoid commute hours. Another possiblitity is to arrange a shuttle from the airport to Franklin (call 615/275-1675 for airport transportation information) or check with one of the Franklin motels. Once outside of Franklin, TN 96 offers wide paved shoulders for the 9-mile trip to the Parkway.

Sometimes a friendly person at a bike shop can arrange (for a fee) to give you a lift between the Natchez Trace Parkway and the airport at Jackson or Nashville. The bus station in Natchez also arranges shuttles to the Jackson and Baton Rouge airports.

Bus—Greyhound Trailways provides service to Natchez, Jackson, Tupelo, and Nashville, plus smaller towns such as Kosciusko, Florence, and Franklin. The bus trip between Nashville and Natchez runs through Memphis and takes approximately 13 hours. Bikes must be boxed so you need to call a bike shop and ask them to hold a box for you. In some cases, cyclists have improvised bike boxes by taping together several pieces of flattened cardboard. The bus station in Nashville is located on 8th Ave S. just south of Broadway and is a short walk from various downtown hotels. The Natchez station is two miles away from the downtown area at the intersection of Lower Woodville Rd. and John Junkin Dr. (also US 65, 84, and 98).

Greyhound/Trailways Phone Numbers
Nationwide 800/231-2222
Natchez 601/445-5291   Tupelo 662/842-4557
Jackson 601/353-6342   Nashville 615/255-3508
Rental Vehicles—For groups of three or more, renting a car one way from Nashville to Jackson or Baton Rouge may be cheaper (and more convenient) than taking the bus. Currently, no rental companies allow drop-offs in Natchez. You will probably need to arrange to have your bikes shipped if you opt to rent a car. U-haul (800/789-3638) and Ryder (800/467-9337) rent trucks one way between Nashville and Natchez, and some dealers can store your car while you travel the Trace.

Rental Bikes—Bike shops (see *Appendices*) near the Trace may rent quality bikes. Occasionally road touring bikes are available, but mountain bikes are most common. If you rent a mountain bike, ask that slick tires be installed—this will save wasted energy plus the annoyance of whining knobby tires on pavement. I suggest you learn what size bike you need and then make rental arrangements in advance.

Shipping—I have shipped our bikes via UPS on several occasions and found it to be less expensive and more convenient than flying with them. Plus, you can insure your bike which you can't with the airlines. Bikes still must be boxed carefully to ensure no damage occurs. For a fee, bike shops will box and ship your bike—a very worthwhile investment upon ending a tour. Ann and I would much rather go out on the town rather than spend 1-2 hours boxing our bikes and then try to get them to a UPS location. Bike shops will also receive and assemble plus repair anything that may have been damaged during shipping. Although the shops near the Trace offer these services, you should definately call to make advance arrangements. Once when I stopped into the Natchez Bicycle Center, owner Frank Moak had ten bikes to be boxed and shipped.

USING THIS GUIDE

This guide divides the Natchez Trace Parkway into six sections based on landmarks or cities along the Trace. The *Jackson Bypass* detours an unfinished portion of the Parkway, and routes into Nashville and Natchez are also included. Service listings are based on the milepost markers along the Parkway which makes it relatively simple to plan a day's journey. The chapters listed under *Touring the Trace* start in Natchez and follow the milepost numbers which increase as you head north. (Southbound cyclists will need to work backwards from specific mileposts.)

Once you are aquainted with a few logical abbreviations, it will be easy to find the services you need. Directions and distances to various services are included; only distances are included for B&Bs. Since you will be thinking in terms of going north or south, services are listed as east or west of the Parkway although some highways may actually run north to south.

Elevation information is based on an Avocet altimeter watch I wore while both cycling and driving the Parkway. In other words, these numbers are estimations—not geological surveys. Nevertheless, they provide a reliable indication on how hilly each section is. The numbers listed indicate the difference between the lowest and highest point, the total (or accumulated) vertical gain, and the average accumulated climb per mile during the entire segment.

OVERNIGHT TOURS and DAY RIDES

The maps included with these rides are based on county maps and include several local roads in addition to major highways. Even so, staying on course can be a challenge since street signs are sometimes non-existent or turned the wrong way. In cities and towns, a few of the roads on a route may not be labeled on the map, but they will be in the directions. By using *both* the maps and the written directions, you will be able to follow these routes even in areas where the road signs are missing. Watch for hints in the written directions, such as "stop sign at the T-intersection," "first right," or "at the top of a hill" to help you stay on course. ALWAYS READ THE NEXT DIRECTION AHEAD OF TIME SO YOU WON'T MISS A TURN AND THEN WONDER WHERE YOU ARE!!!

Several rides have two or more options of varying lengths, all of which share some of the same route. For example, this could allow you to ride 15 miles and then decide whether you feel like taking the 25-mile option or the 35-mile option. Be sure to read the italicized print at the end of each option to find where your route continues in the printed directions.

Key to Abbreviations:

W	Water
RR	Restroom
PS	Picnic Shelter
Mkt	Market
Rst	Restaurant
Supermkt	Supermarket
Cpg	Campground
Ldg	Lodging (Motels and B&Bs)
$	Lodging under $75
$$	Lodging between $75-125
$$$	Lodging over $125
mp	Milepost
CR	County Road
TN, AL, or MS	State Highway
US	Federal Highway
NTP	Natchez Trace Parkway

NATCHEZ TO NATCHEZ TRACE PARKWAY

Highlights: Downtown Natchez, Natchez-Under-the-Hill, Isle of Capri Casino, Fort Rosalie, Grand Village of the Natchez, Natchez Museum of African-American History, Emerald Mound, Historic homes (at least 14 homes open year-round for tours, many more are open during the Spring, Fall, and Christmas Pilgrimages).
Terrain: Rolling.
Lodging: Nearly 40 B&Bs available in Natchez plus several motels.

No other city preserves the wealth and grandeur of the Old South like Natchez. The reason Natchez became a wealthy town is no mystery. It was the final destination for thousands of flatboats and the beginning of the overland trek home for the boatmen. After use of the Trace declined, the town continued to prosper as a major cotton port for the nearby plantations. Many of these exquisitely grand homes served as "town homes" of the regional planters who often had one or more plantations in the country.

When visiting these houses, keep in perspective that fewer than 25% of white Southerners were members of families that owned slaves and less than 12% owned more than 20 slaves. Although only 1% held more than 100 slaves, the majority of slaves lived on these large plantations. So you can see that these stately mansions belonged to a very small elite class, and the majority of white Southerners did not prosper from the injustices of slavery.

Stanton Hall

Partly due to the large number of Union sympathizers in town, Natchez fell without a shot during the Civil War. Consequently, it was not ravaged and burned like other less-fortunate towns in the South. After the war, the town's prosperity declined along with the cotton economy. With no money to modernize, the hundreds of historic structures were spared from demolition. In recent years, many homes have been carefully restored, and the past's misfortunes have evolved into a new tourism boom today.

When the French arrived in the early 1700s, only the small Natchez Tribe maintained the mound building ways of Mississippian people. Their culture, considered the most advance in the Southeast, resembled the Aztecs and Mayas of Central and South America. Their chief, or Great Sun, held absolute control over his people which were divided into the classes of suns, nobles, honored people, and stinkards (commoners). The Great Sun could marry only stinkards, and his wives were slain upon his death to accompany him in the afterlife. Besides the great mound building feats of these people, their pottery, tool making, and farming were advanced as well.

In 1703, Jean Penicaut, a French carpenter who came here with the Iberville expedition, wrote "We paid visit to the Natchez, one of the most polite and affable nations on the Mississippi. The Natchez inhabit one of the most beautiful countries in Louisiana (as it was then called)... and is embellished with magnificent natural scenery, covered with a splendid growth of odoriferous trees and plants, and watered with cool and limpid streams. This nation is composed of thirty villages, but the one we visited was the largest, because it contained the dwelling of the Great Chief, who they called the Sun."

Today the site of the **Grand Village** visited by Penicaut is preserved by the state of Mississippi. It is located approximately three miles southeast of downtown on Jefferson Davis Blvd. A visitor center containing artifacts and other displays is adjacent to the village site where only the eroded mounds remain.

Emerald Mound, situated near the Parkway, stands as the most impressive structure of the Plaquemine culture which was the southern region of the Mississippian culture. Used from 1200 A.D. to 1700 A.D., this 35-foot high flat-top mound covers eight acres and is the second largest ceremonial mound in the country. Two secondary mounds (the west one is 30 feet high) sit on top of the large mound. When Ann and I stood on the west mound as the sun was setting, we noticed our shadows casting a line directly toward the other small mound.

In 1716, the French asserted their claim to the entire Mississippi Valley by constructing Fort Rosalie on a high bluff along the river in present day Natchez. The Natchez Indians rebelled 13 years later and massacred the isolated settlement. Their victory was short lived for the French struck back and annihilated the entire tribe. Over the next

130 years, the flags of five nations would fly over this fair town on the river bluff. (See p. 13 for additional history of the Natchez region.)

Natchez today stands as a jewel at the end of the Trace—ready to rejuvenate the weary cyclists. With nearly 40 bed & breakfasts and numerous motels and restaurants, this town easily accommodates its self-propelled visitors. The 1920s style Natchez Eola Hotel and several historic B&Bs are located in the heart of town. From any of these places it is easy to walk (or bike) to the numerous restaurants and the historic homes. You can ride the trolley or take a horse drawn carriage if you simply have no energy left in your legs to go out on the town. For those desiring to stay in a grand old plantation home in a rural setting, several first class B&Bs are situated only a few miles from Natchez. The **Natchez Visitors Reception Center** (near the bridge on US 84 and Canal St.) will help you plan your visit, plus you can relax while viewing the 20-minute "The Natchez Story."

By heading down Silver Street you will find yourself along the Mississippi River at **Natchez-Under-the-Hill**. In the boatmen days, this place was notorious for saloons, gambling, and prostitution. It is said that more than a few Kaintucks started their long journey home with no money remaining from the goods they had sold. Restaurants and bars still do a brisk business today, and you are more than welcomed to lose all of your money at the **Isle of Capri Casino**—open 24 hours, every day of the year!

A trip to Natchez wouldn't be complete without touring a few of the gracious homes in this town that was once the richest place in the South. The concept of touring antebellum homes began in 1932 when Natchez hosted the National Garden Club Convention. Unfortunately, a late frost ruined the local gardens. Not to be defeated, the resourceful ladies of the Natchez Garden Club decided to rejuvenate several historic houses and conduct tours. Now, thousands of tourists visit during the pilgrimages in October, December, and

April when many of the beautifully restored homes are open to the public.

For year-round tours in the downtown area, the **Linden** (1800)**, Magnolia Hall** (1858)**, Stanton Hall** (1857), and the **House on Ellicott's Hill** (1798), top the list. My personal favorite is **Rosalie**, located on the bluff above Natchez-Under-the-Hill. Originally the site of Ft. Rosalie, this gracious 1820s mansion served as the Union headquarters during the Civil War. From here, a short walk north on Broadway leads to a small picturesque park affording great views of the Mississippi River. You may also want to tour the **William Johnson Complex** on State St. which was the home of a successful African-American freeman known as the Barber of Natchez.

Longwood, located two miles from downtown, (go east on Orleans St. which becomes Homochitto St., then Lower Woodville Rd.) stands as one of the most elegant and unique homes in this architectural mecca. But looks can be deceiving—this 1860s Oriental style octagonal house was never finished. The workers, mostly from the North, fled town at

Longwood

the beginning of the Civil War. The family's fortune soon declined, and the interior was never completed. They continued to live in the basement while the upstairs remained untouched with its "temporary" cypress floors littered with tools left by the workmen.

Also within two miles of downtown, **Melrose**, an 1845 Greek Revival home, shares the spacious grounds with several outbuildings including slave cabins that currently contain one of the few slavery exhibits in the country. Several photographs and journals describe how the field slave often worked as many as 17 hours a day in sweltering conditions.

In May of 2005, the Trace was completed to the Southern Terminus which is only 2 miles from downtown Natchez. The ride into town is reasonably pleasant, but you should try to avoid commuting hours if possible. If time permits, stop by the Melrose Plantation which is only a short detour south on Melrose Ave. Also, be sure to admire the impressive Monmouth Plantation, now an elegant B&B, on your way to or from Natchez.

Mississippi Queen leaving Natchez

Call the Natchez Convention & Visitors Bureau at 800/634-1818 or visit www.visitnatchez.com for a complete listing of restaurants, accommodations, and attractions.

Natchez Restaurants

Biscuits & Blues—315 Main St. (lunch and dinner, closed Mon.) Seafood, smoked meats, and Eggplant Orleans.

Bowie's Tavern—100 Main St. Mon. - Fri. 4-9; Sat. & Sun. 11-10) Named after Jim Bowie whose famous duel happened near Natchez, this tavern serves a varied menu from andouille sausage po-boys to black bean pizza.

Cock of the Walk—200 N. Broadway (daily 5 -?)A great place to enjoy fried catfish and hush puppies while watching the sunset over the big river.

The City Cafe—109 N. Pearl St. (Mon.-Fri. 7:30-5:00; Sat 8-2) Breakfast plates plus soups, salads, and deli sandwiches for lunch. Don't forget the homemade desserts!

Fat Mama's Tamales—500 Canal St. (open daily) A taste of Mexico in a modest yet colorful atmosphere.

King's Tavern—619 Jefferson St. (Mon.-Sat. 11:30-2, 5-10; Sun. 5-10) Currently a steak house specializing in hickory smoked prime rib, this tavern was built in the 1780s on the Natchez Trace and served as a stagecoach stop and mail station.

Magnolia Grill—Natchez Under the Hill (Mon.-Sat. 11-10; Sun. 11-4:30) Popular spot for locals and those visiting the casino.

Main St. Market Place Cafe—Main St. and Rankin St. (Mon.-Sat. 7-2; Sun 8-12)

Pearl Street Pasta—105 Pearl St. (Mon.-Sat. lunch/dinner; Sun. dinner) Located in the heart of town, this is a great place to carbo load. Healthy menu includes vegetarian meals.

Pig-Out Inn—166 S. Canal St. (lunch and dinner) Popular place for barbecue lovers.

Planet Thailand—116 N. Commerce (Mon.-Sat. lunch & dinner) Certainly a change of pace from traditional southern cooking.

Natchez Eola—Pearl St. and Main St. (breakfast, lunch, dinner) Elegant dining at Julep's and casual dining at the Peacock Bar & Grill.

Stanton Hall/Carriage House Restaurant—401 High St. (11-2:30; dinner served during Spring and Fall Pilgrimages) Elegant dining in one of the most beautiful historic homes in Natchez. Famous for its fried chicken. (Reservations recommended, 601/445-5151)

Downtown Lodging

Aunt Frannie's $$ (601/446-9685) Gothic style 1850s home on Union St..

Bluff Top $$ (601/304-1002 or 800/211-6420) Enjoy a room with a river view in an 1890s Victorian Queen Ann B&B, all within a short walk to the downtown restaurants.

The Burn $$-$$$ (601/442-1344 or 800/654-8859) One of the earliest (1836) Greek Revival homes in Natchez is located along our route on Union St.

The Doctor's In $$$ (601-442-3561) Colonial Revival home furnished with antiques.

Guest House Historic Hotel $$-$$$ (601/442-1054 or 888/442-4425) This 1840s three story hotel with 18 rooms has been converted into a charming B&B in the heart of downtown.

Highpoint $$-$$$(800/283-4099 or 601/442-6963) Victorian Country Manor on the river bluff.

Mark Twain Guesthouse $-$$ (601/446-8023) Relive the boatmen days in a room above a saloon at Natchez -Under-the-Hill. Don't expect quiet on a weekend night!

Miss Lucy's Cottage $$$ (601/446-6631) Private victorian cottage with lovely garden located on State St. Full kitchen.

Myrtle Corner $$-$$$ (601/445-5999) Lovely pink and white 1890s Colonial Revival Townhouse with private courtyard.

Natchez Eola Hotel $$ (866/445-EOLA or 601/445-6000) This 1920s hotel with a beautiful lobby with marble floors, elegant furnishings, and original chandeliers is the tallest building in the historic district.

Natchez Historic Inn $$-$$$ (601/442-8848 or 866/442-8848) Built in 1844, this inn features 17 rooms furnished with antiques.

Pleasant Hill $$-$$$ (601/442-7674) 1835 Greek Revival home with spacious porches and breezeway in the heart of the historic district.

Riverside B&B $$-$$$ (601/446-5730) Built circa 1858, this 3-guestroom house offers excellent views of the mighty Mississippi and is a short walk to Natchez Under the Hill and other attractions. We thoroughly enjoyed our stay (and gourmet breakfast!) in this out-of-the-way B&B.

Wensel House $$ (601/445-8577 or 888/775-8577) 1888 Victorian mansion featuring turn-of-the-century antiques.

Lodging Outside of Town

The Briars B&B $$$ (601/446-9654 or 800/634-1818) Built circa 1815, this home overlooking the river was the site of Jefferson Davis's wedding.
Comfort Inn $-$$ (601/446-5500 or 800/221-2222) Located 1 mile northeast of town on US 61 near Wilson Rd. Pool.
Dunleith $$ (601/446-8500 or 800/433-2445) Magnificent 1856 Greek Revival home with white columns on every side. Located 1 mile south of town on Homochitto St.
Isle of Capri Casino Hotel $$ (800/722-LUCK or 601/445-0605) Located near the Mississippi River bridge, this modern hotel is a 10-20 minute walk to the downtown attractions. Jacuzzi and pool.
Monmouth B&B $$$ (601/442-5852 or 800/828-4531) Rated one of the top ten romantic places, this grand mansion sits on 35 acres. Only 2 miles away from downtown.
Natchez Inn $ (601/442-0221) Most economical lodging near downtown. Only a 20 minute walk to the historic section.
Oakland B&B $$ (601/445-5101 or 800/824-0355) Located 8 miles south of town on 360 acres, the 1785 guest house is the oldest brick home in the state.
Ramada Inn Hilltop $$ (601/446-6311 or 800/256-6311) Located by the Mississippi River Bridge, only a 10-20 minute walk to the downtown attractions. Pool.
Weymouth B&B $$-$$$ (601/445-2304) 1855 Greek Revival home situated on a high bluff above the river 1 mile north of town. Spectacular sunsets.

Natchez to Natchez Trace Parkway (Northbound)

0.0   Begin milage at State St. and Dr. M.L. King Blvd. Continue biking east (away fromt he river) on State St. which becomes J.A. Quitman Blvd. King Blvd. is also part of the MississippiRiver Trail.

0.9   Cross Melrose Ave. Street now becomes Liberty Rd.

1.9   Go under Sgt. Prentiss Dr./US 61 & 84. Supermarket and motels within one mile to the north on Sgt. Prentiss Dr.

2.1   **Right** onto Natchez Trace Parkway.

Natchez Trace Parkway to Natchez (Southbound)

0.0   Exit the Parkway heading toward Natchez and merge onto Liberty Rd.

0.3   Go under Sgt. Prentiss Dr./US 61 & 84. Supermarket and motels within one mile to the north on Sgt. Prentiss Dr.

1.2   Bear **left** as you approach Melrose Ave. You will actually be on Franklin St. and Quitman Blvd. very briefly, but you will ultimately end up on Main St.

2.2   Cross Dr. M.L. King Blvd. You are now in downtown Natchez. King Blvd. is also part of the Mississippi River Trail. Tourist information available at 521 Main St.

Western Auto Store (**Bike Shop**) *(601/445-4186), located a half mile south of Liberty Rd. on Sgt. Prentiss Dr., provides bike parts and repair and will package and ship bikes.*

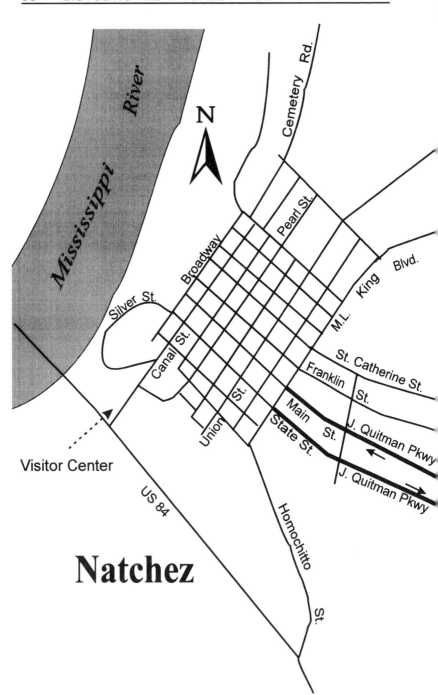

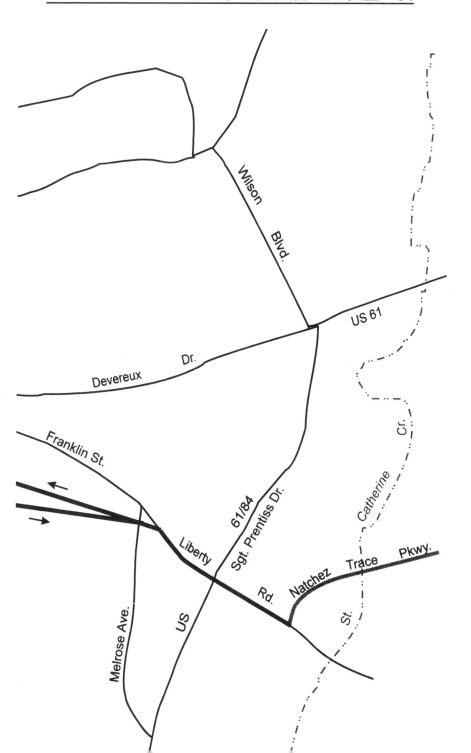

SOUTHERN TERMINUS
TO JACKSON
mp 1-83

Highlights: Emerald Mound, Loess Bluff, Mount Locust, Springfield Plantation, Port Gibson, Sunken Trace, Grindstone Ford/Magnum Site, Owens Creek Waterfall, Rocky Springs, Lower Choctaw Boundary, Dean's Stand, Battle of Raymond.

Terrain: Several short, but challenging hills south of Port Gibson becoming flat-to-rolling north of Bayou Pierre.

Northbound Elevation: 300 ft. difference; 1,940 ft. accumulated; 24 ft. average per mile.

Southbound Elevation: 300 ft. difference; 1,940 ft. accumulated; 24 ft. average per mile.

Camping: Natchez Trace State Park (mp 10), Rocky Springs (mp 55).

Lodging: Natchez Trace State Park (mp 10), Jim's Cabin (mp 20), Rosswood B&B (mp 30), Port Gibson (mp 38 and 41), Raymond (mp 79).

This is the Deep South! Only down here will you find Spanish moss hanging from the trees along the Parkway. The scenery varies from hardwood forest hosting various plants and trees found in the subtropics to open pastures and cotton fields. Several grand plantation homes dating back to the late 1700s are within 2-6 miles of the Parkway. Some of these homes are charming bed and breakfasts where you can pamper yourself in the traditions of the Old South. The day rides, the *Church Hill Loop* and the *Windsor Ruins Loop*, give all the details for finding these relics of the past.

Earlier travelers didn't enjoy the luxuries of these B&Bs, but they were still grateful for the accommodations at **Mt. Locust**, the only restored stand along the Natchez

Mt. Locust

Trace. Park Service interpreters offer free tours of the rooms furnished with original antiques from various periods of the inn's history. John Blommart, one of the wealthiest men in the Natchez District, built Mt. Locust in 1779 on a land grant from the British. Blommart unsuccessfully led a military campaign against the Spanish who later acquired the Natchez territory. Because of his actions, the Spanish imprisoned Blommart and confiscated his land.

In 1784, William Ferguson purchased Mt. Locust and soon found many Kaintucks knocking on his door asking for provisions and a place to sleep. Numerous boatmen spent the first night of their homeward journey on his porch. Soon Ferguson added several rooms, an upstairs, and an annex called "Sleepy Hollow" to provide shelter for the travelers.

Cyclists will encounter numerous hills between Natchez and Port Gibson. These **Loess Hills** form a 2 to

30-mile wide formation along the east bank of the Mississippi River between Baton Rouge and Memphis. They were formed in the last Ice Age during a nearly continuous dust storm that swept in from the western plains. Since the earliest white settlement, this loose topsoil, occasionally up to 100 feet deep, formed deep gullies as horses and wagons eroded the soil on local roads such as the Natchez Trace. This erosion is best seen on the **Sunken Trace** just north of Port Gibson. While walking along this sunken path under a canopy of trees draped with Spanish moss, it is not hard to imagine a lone horseman appearing around the bend on his wilderness journey.

It would be a shame to bike the Trace without visiting **Port Gibson**, the town General Grant said was "too beautiful to burn." This chapter includes a brief detour from the Parkway that leads to all the local services and the gracious antebellum homes on Church Street before returning to the Parkway four miles from where you got off. Be sure to notice the First Presbyterian Church's unusual steeple with a gold finger pointing skyward. The original finger was erected in 1859 in honor of Reverend Butler who frequently pointed to the heavens during his sermons. We enjoyed walking along the shaded sidewalks of Church Street and stopping to read the markers in front of the historical homes. Afterwards, we spent the night at the grandest home of all, the Greek Revival **Oak Square Plantation** (1850), which is now an elegant bed & breakfast. The original grounds, with gardens and dependencies, occupied an entire city block. Another bed & breakfast and a motel also offer shelter for the modern day traveler. The **Allen Collection**, featuring photographs of the rural South in the early 1900s, can be seen at the City Hall on Orange Street.

The **Rocky Springs** site preserves the grounds of a town established in the 1790s that has long vanished. By 1860, the local cotton economy was thriving, and the town supported three merchants, four physicians, four teachers, three clergy, and thirteen artisans. 54 planters and 28 over-seers lived on the surrounding farmland. But the real reason for the town's prosperity was the more than 2,000 slaves who tended the cotton. Perhaps the town was most notorious for the Red House Tavern which is marked by a crumbling cistern along the nature trail. In its day, many outlaws in-cluding the brutal Harpe Brothers and the Mason Gang fre-quented this place while using a nearby hideout. An unsolved murder took place near the spring during the hey-day of these bandits who were greatly feared by honest travelers. During the Civil War, there is no doubt the Union soldiers marching to Jackson received icy stares from the local inhabitants.

After the Civil War, the plantation economy began to decline. In 1878, a yellow fever epidemic spread through the town. The boll weevil, an insect that devastated the Deep South, destroyed the remaining cotton fields in the early 1900s. By the 1930s, the last store closed its door and the forest gradually replaced the town. Only the Rocky Springs Church remains. A one-mile uphill spur road leads to the townsite where interpretive markers explain the history of the town.

If you are camping here and are in need of a refreshing shower, go south for one-half mile to the **Owens Creek Waterfall** and stand under the cool water—a real treat in hot weather! Although the sign says it is usually dry, it was flowing the three times I visited.

Port Gibson Restaurants

Old Depot Restaurant—S. Market St. which parallels US 61 on the west side (Mon.-Sat. 11-10) Located in the old train station, the reasonably-priced meals at this popular establishment include fried chicken, fried catfish, steak, seafood, po'boy sandwiches, and Cajun food.

JB's Restaurant—Market St. (Mon.-Sat. 7:30 a.m.-7 p.m.) Plain and simple down-home cookin' at bargain prices.

Grant's Place—just north of town on US 61 (Mon.-Sat. 10-9; Sun. 10-5) A meat n' three with good food at great prices.

Sunken Trace at mp 41.5

Milepost
4.8	Elizabeth Female Academy. Mississippi's first female college operated here from 1818 to 1845. It's most notable graduate was Varina Davis, wife of Confederate President Jefferson Davis.
8.0	US 61
10.3	Emerald Mound/MS 553 (**Ldg**, **Cpg**). This impressive flat top mound of the Mississippian era is the second largest ceremonial mound in the United States. The mound is 1 mi. (and a minor hill) off the Parkway. Natchez State Park (601/442-2658), with cabins and camping (showers), is 2 mi. off the Trace by going east on MS 553, crossing US 61, and following the signs to cabins or campground.
12.1	Turpin Creek Picnic Area.
12.4	Loess Bluff. This bare embankment shows the highly erodable Loess Soil that was blown here during the last Ice Age.
15.5	Mt. Locust (**W**, **RR**). Park Service interpreters explain the history of this restored stand. There is also a small bookstore.
17.5	Coles Creek Picnic Area (**W**, **RR**).
18.4	Bullen Creek Nature Trail
20.2	MS 553/Springfield Plantation. (**Ldg**) This elegant plantation home (1780s) was the wedding site of Andrew and Rachel Jackson. It is located 2 mi. west of the Parkway on MS 552 south. Tours available (601/786-3802). Jim's Cabin Rental $$ (601/ 442-1456) is 6 mi. west on this lightly-traveled road. Shuttle service available.
21.7	Mud Island Picnic Area
23.6	North Fork Coles Creek Picnic Area
30.4	MS 552 (**Mkt**, **Ldg**) The often-photographed Lorman 1874 Country Store is located 2 mi. away by going east on MS 552, then south US 61. The Rosswood B&B $$$ (601/437-4215 or 800/533-5889) is 5 mi. east.

37.5   US 61/Port Gibson (**Mkt, Supermkt, Rst, Ldg, Laundry**). See *Port Gibson Optional Detour.*

41.3   MS 18/Port Gibson (**Mkt, Supermkt, Rst, Ldg, Laundry**). See *Port Gibson Optional Detour.*

41.5   Sunken Trace. Centuries of foot and horse travel gradually sunk this portion of the Trace 20 ft. deep into the Loess Soil.

45.7   Grindstone Ford/Magnum Site. A five minute walk follows the Old Trace, passing a pioneer cemetery, to the ford of Bayou Pierre which marked the end of the Natchez District and the beginning of the wilderness and Indian Territory. Excavations of Magnum Mound have revealed evidence of a elaborate religious-oriented society sustained largely through agriculture.

52.4   Owens Creek Waterfall. This small waterfall plunging over a rock house (cliff overhang) is often only a trickle in recent years, but over a century ago it was a popular spot for the residents of Rocky Springs to escape the summer heat.

54.8   Rocky Springs (**W, RR, Cpg**). A small visitor center (usually unstaffed) with water and restrooms is adjacent to the Parkway. The campground is within 1/2 mi. A 1-mile spur road leads uphill to the site of the vanished community of Rocky Springs. **Last reliable water northbound for 34 miles.**

59.1   Fisher Ferry Road (**Mkt**). A country store with a fair selection of non-perishable goods is 1 mi. west of the Parkway.

61.0   Lower Choctaw Boundary/Red Bluff Stand. The boundary of present day Hinds and Clairborne counties previously served as the boundary between the Choctaws and three different nations, France, Spain, and the U.S. Beginning in 1802, John Gregg operated a stand along this boundary where "he keeps on hand a large and general supply of groceries, ground coffee ready to put up, sugar biscuits, teas, cheese, dried beef or bacon, and every other article necessary for the accommodation of travelers going through the nation, on very reasonable terms. He is also prepared to shoe horses on the very shortest notice."

73.5   Dean's Stand. This stand was established in 1820 after this area was open to white settlement. Gen. Grant made his headquarters here after the Battle of Raymond.

76.0   Mamie's Cottage B&B $$ (**Ldg**) (601/857-6051 or 877/629-6051). Quaint cottage located next to historic Dupree House. Guests may walk off the Parkway to reach lodging.

78.3   Battle of Raymond. On May 8, 1863, Gen. Grant's troops clashed with the Confederate brigade of Brig. Gen. John Gregg near the town of Raymond. This convinced Grant of the need to take Jackson in order to assure success in his forthcoming siege of Vicksburg.

79.1   MS 467 (**Mkt, Rst, Ldg**) Markets and restaurants are 3 miles away in Raymond. Oak Hill B$B $$ (601/857-4268) and Cedarwood B&B $$$ (601/857-0690). *Note: Southbound travelers may use Airport Rd. (mp 82.6). Go east and then south on Raymond-Clinton Rd. Return to the Trace via MS 467. Northbound travelers may also save 6 miles by taking MS 467 into town and then heading north on Raymond Clinton Rd. and then go left on Airport Rd.*

89.0   Clinton Visitor Center/Pinehaven Rd. (**W, RR, Mkt, Supermkt, Rst, Ldg, Laundry**). See Jackson chapter for details. **Last reliable water southbound for 34 miles.**

Port Gibson Lodging

Visit www.portgibsononthemississippi.com or 601/437-4351
Bernheimer House $$-$$$ (601/437-2843)
Collina Plantation $$$ (601/437-5434
Grand Gulf Inn $ (601/437-8811)
Oak Square Plantation B&B $$-$$$ (601/437-4350 or 800/729-0240)

Port Gibson Optional Detour (Northbound)

Mile

0.0   Exit onto US 61 at mp 37.4.

0.2   **Left** on US 61 at the end of the access road.

0.3   **Right** on Bridewell Ln. before going under the NTP.

1.8   Cross MS 594 (stop sign).

2.3   **Left** on Magnolia St. (becomes Greenwood St.) after passing a factory on the right.

2.8   **Right** on Church St./US 61 at the stop sign

3.3   Orange St. (**Supermkt, Rst, Laundry**). The Old Restaurants and a large supermarket are located on Market St. two blocks west from this intersection.

3.8   **Right** on MS 18 at the traffic light (**Mkt, Rst**).

5.0   **Left** on NTP access road.

5.3   **Left** on Natchez Trace going north.

Port Gibson Optional Detour (Southbound)

Mile

0.0   Exit onto MS 18 at mp 41.3.

0.3   **Right** on MS 18 at the end of the access road.

1.4   **Left** on Church St./US 61 at the light (**Mkt, Rst**).

1.9   Cross Orange St. (**Supermkt, Rst, Laundry**). Restaurants and a large supermarket are located on Market Street two blocks west from this intersection.

2.5   **Left** on Greenwood St. (becomes Magnolia St.).

3.0   **Right** on Bridewell Ln. (stop sign at the T-intersection).

3.4   Cross MS 594 (stop sign).

5.1   **Left** on US 61 (stop sign at T-intersection).

5.2   **Right** at the entrance to the Parkway.

5.4   **Left** on the NTP going south.

THE JACKSON SECTION
Clinton to Ridgeland

mp 89-102

Highlights on the Trace: Clinton Visitor Center,
Cowles Meade Cemetery, Osburn Stand, Choctaw
Agency, Mississippi Crafts Center.
Highlights in Jackson: LeFleur Bluff State Park, Jim
Buck Ross Agricultural and Forestry Museum, Old
Capitol Museum, Governor's Mansion, Oaks
House, Manship House.
Terrain: Mostly flat.
Camping: Clinton (mp 89).
Lodging: Clinton (mp 89) and Ridgeland (mp 102).

In 1789, French Canadian Louis LeFleur established a
trading post on Choctaw land along the Pearl River known
as LeFleur's Bluff. Only 31 years later, it was selected to
become the capital of the new state of Mississippi. In May
of 1863, General Grant's troops set the young city afire
earning Jackson the nickname of Chimneyville.

Today, **Downtown Jackson** offers metropolitan excite-
ment for the cyclist willing to pedal the busy streets to get
there. Sue Pitts, former Mississippi Bicycle Coordinator,
provided much of this route into downtown. Even if you
avoid peak traffic hours, cycling to downtown Jackson is
only for those accustomed to riding in traffic. Another option
is to stay at one of the motels in Ridgeland and take a bus
or taxi for the 9 mile journey downtown. However you
manage to get there, Jackson offers plenty to do, while
providing a refreshing contrast to the miles of rural Mississippi you've been enjoying.

Highlights of the **Downtown Walking Tour** (available from the Visitor Bureau) include the Old Capitol (1830) which is now a state museum, the new State Capitol (1903), the Governor's Mansion (1842), and two lovely restored homes—the Oaks House and Manship House, both of which survived the Civil War. For those seeking charming and elegant accommodations within walking distance of these sights, consider staying at the **Millsaps Buie House**, the **Poindexter Park Inn B&B**, or the **Old Capitol Inn** (see next page). Several hotels are also located in downtown Jackson.

For those on a budget, camping is possible only five miles northeast of downtown at **LeFleur's Bluff State Park** on Lakeland Drive just east of I-55. Once again, cycling this busy four lane highway is not for the faint of heart. Across the street is the **Jim Buck Ross Mississippi Agricultural and Forestry Museum** exhibiting an 1860s farmstead and a 1920s version of Small Town, Mississippi.

For those going downtown or to LeFleur Bluff State Park, we highly recommend obtaining a city map when you get here or call the Visitors Bureau (see *Appendices*) for a free map and a list of accommodations and attractions.

The section of the Natchez Trace Parkway which skirts Jackson from the suburbs of Clinton to Ridgeland was completed in May of 2005. Due to traffic, the Park Service strongly suggests that cyclists avoid the Trace during the morning and afternoon commuting hours as well as weekend afternoons. It is sad that Park Service discourages visiting a national park due to commuters who do not respect the rights of cyclists. Still, it is probably wise to heed their advice. A 5-mile paved path parallels the Trace from mp 101 to mp 106 allowing bicyclists to escape the somtimes busy traffic and find services (see pp. 68 & 78).

For a complete listing of accommodations, restaurants, attractions, and a street map, call the Jackson Visitors Bureau at 601/960-1891 or 800/354-7695 or visit www.visitjackson.com

Lodging
Some B&B's will providce a shuttle. Call to inquire.

Millsaps Buie House $$$ (800/784-0221) 1888 home located in the heart of Jackson.
Fairview Inn $$$ (888-948-1203) 1908 mansion with large gardens located near the bike route into Jackson.
The Poindexter Park Inn B&B $$ (601/944-1392), built in 1907, is located near the central business district and Capital City sites. They offer shuttle service to guests from the Parkway and the airport.
Old Capitol Inn $$-$$$ (601/359-9000) An historicYWCA building converted into a charming B&B next to the state capitol.

Clinton Lodging
www.clintonms.org or 601/924-5912

Clinton Inn $ (601/924-5313) On US 80 just east of Spring Ridge Rd.
Econolodge $-$$ (601/924-9364) Spring Ridge Rd. near I-20.
Quality Inn $$ (601/924-0064) Spring Ridge Rd. near I-20.
Days Inn $-$$ (601/925-5065) Spring Ridge Rd. near I-20.

Ridgeland Lodging
www.visitridgeland.com or 800/468-6078

Cabot Lodge $ (601/957-0757) On Dyess Rd., take E. Frontage Rd. south from Center St.
Days Inn $-$$ (601/956-9726 or 800/DAYSINN) On Center St. west of Ridgewood Rd.
Red Roof Inn $ (601/956-7707 or 800/843-7663) E. Frontage Rd. near Center St.
Quality Inn $$ (601/957-6203) Ridgewood Rd. near Center St.

Milepost

89.0   Clinton Visitor Center/Pinehaven Rd. (**W, RR, Mkt, Rst, Ldg, Cpg, Supermkt, Laundry**). The visitor center is adjacent to the parkway exit. A market/restaurant is just east of the Parkway toward Clinton. Additional services are located in Clinton 1-3 miles south of the Trace.

Directions into Clinton

0.0   Go south (east) on Pinehaven Rd.

0.4   Northside Dr. Supermarket, restaurants, and coin laundry are a half mile to the left on Northside Dr.

To reach motels, cross Northside Dr. and continue a very short distance on Clinton Pkwy. Then go:

0.5   **Right** on Cynthia Rd.

0.7   **Left** on Monroe St. (traffic light).

1.6   **Left** on W. College St. at the entrance to Mississippi College (traffic light).

1.8   **Right** on Clinton Pkwy./Spring Ridge Rd.

2.5   Motels and RV Park and located near I-20

You can also use Clinton Pkwy. rather than Monroe St., but Monroe St. makes a nice diversion thru the old part of town and by the historic Mississippi College.

88.0   Cowles Mead Cemetery. Cowles Mead ran a tavern on the Trace near Natchez, before becoming acting governor of Mississippi. Later he moved to this location and built his plantation home "Greenwood." After his death, it was burned during the Civil War.

93.2   Hwy. 49 (**Mkt**). One mile south of exit.

95.0   Osburn Stand. Noble Osburn operated an inn here beginning in 1811 under an agreement with the Choctaw Indians.

100.0   Choctaw Agency. Choctaw Agent Silas Dinsmore lived here from 1807 until 1820. As the United States pressured the tribe into ceding more and more land, the agency had to move four times to stay within the shrinking tribal boundaries.

100.8   Ridgland Visitors Center/Multi-use Path (**W, RR, Visitors Center**). Bicyclists may access the visitor center which is just north of the Parkway via a paved path. Northbound bicyclists may opt to escape the traffic for the next 5 miles on a paved multi-use trail which parallels the parkway to the Reservoir Overlook at mp 106. Two spur paths lead to additional services (see below and p. 78)

102.4   US 51/Parkway Information Center (**W, RR, Visitors Center, PS, Mkt, Rst, Ldg, Supermkt, Bike Shop**). A large supermarket is .3 mi. south toward Jackson on US 51. Several motels (see Ridgeland Lodging) and restaurants are located 1 mi. south on US 51 then left for .5 mi. on Ridgewood Rd. (Expect fast frequent traffic and no shoulders). Numerous restaurants are also available.

Bike Shop Access

A bike path leads from Parkway Information Center (mp 102.4) to Indian Cycle Fitness & Outdoor Center (601/956-8383). From the parking area, continue through the parking lot and go left on the bike path. In 1/4 mi., take the path to the right which will parallels Pear Orchard Rd. Indian Cycles is 1.5 mi. down this road. A market (snacks) is located a little more than halfway to the shop.

Highway 51 Exit (mp 102) to Downtown Jackson

0.0 From parking area of the Parkway Information Cabin, take the bike path spur along Pear Orchard Rd. (or ride the street if you prefer) to Indian Cycle and Fitness. Continue on Pear Orchard Rd. to County Line Rd. (You may also go straight to Old Canton Rd. but this stretch is narrow with fast traffic.)

1.7 **Left** on Northpark Dr.

2.2 **Right** on Avery Blvd.

2.4 **Left** on E. County Line Rd.

2.8 **Right** on Old Canton Rd.

6.2 **Left**, staying on Old Canton Rd.

6.9 **Right** on Northside Dr. and go under I-55

7.5 **Left** on Manhattan Rd.

7.9 **Left** on Meadowbrook Rd.

8.0 **Right** on Buckley Dr.

8.2 **Left** on Old Canton Ln.

8.4 **Right** on Old Canton Rd.

9.6 **Left** on Lakeland Dr.

9.8 **Right** at traffic light into Mississippi Medical Center

9.9 **Right** on University Ave. att 3-way stop.

10.0 **Left** on Peachtree St. at 4-way stop.

10.3 Peachtree St. ends at Woodrow Wilson Blvd. (Use your best judgement. Cross the street with care, or use the crosswalk one half mile to the west on State St.) Either way continue south on Peachtree St.

10.8 **Right** on Arlington St.

11.0 **Left** on Jefferson St.

11.7 **Right** on Boyd St.

11.8 **Left** on North St.

12.5 Old State Capitol at Amite St. and North St.

Downtown Jackson to Natchez Trace at mp 102

0.0   From the northside of the Old State Capitol, bike north on North St.

0.7   **Right** on Boyd St.

0.8   **Left** on Jefferson St.

1.5   **Right** on Arlington St.

1.7   **Left** on Peachtree St.

2.2   Peachtree St. ends at Woodrow Wilson Blvd. (Use your best judgement. Cross the street with care, or use the crosswalk one half mile to the west on State St.) Either way continue north on Peachtree St.

2.5   **Right** at 4-way stop.

2.6   **Left** at 3-way stop.

2.7   **Left** on Lakeland Dr.

2.9   **Right** on Old Canton Rd.

4.5   **Left** on Meadowbrook Rd.

4.6   **Right** on Manhattan Rd.

5.0   **Right** on Northside Dr. and go under I-55.

5.6   **Left** on Old Canton Rd.

9.7   **Left** on East County Line Rd.

10.1   **Right** on Avery Blvd.

10.3   **Left** on Northpark Dr.

10.8   **Right** on Pear Orchard Rd. (You may also use the adjacent bike path that begins after Indian Cycle and Fitness.)

12.4   Cross Rice Rd. and go left on bike path to the Parkway.

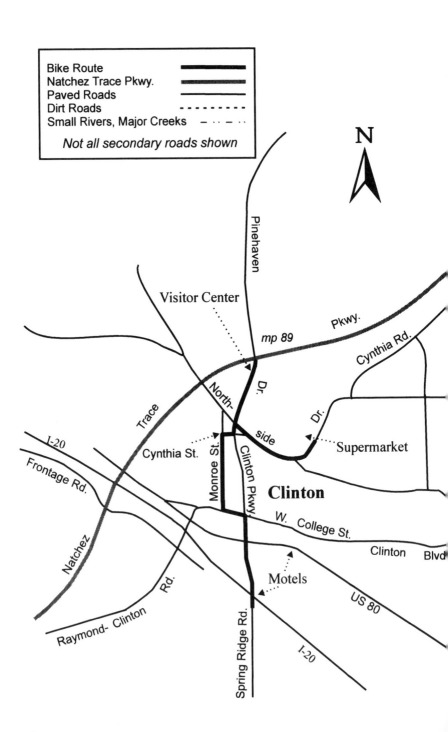

Bike Route
Natchez Trace Pkwy.
Paved Roads
Dirt Roads
Small Rivers, Major Creeks

Not all secondary roads shown

N

Pinehaven

Visitor Center

Pkwy.

mp 89

Cynthia Rd.

North-

Trace

Dr.

side

Dr.

I-20

Cynthia St.

Monroe St.

Clinton Pkwy.

Supermarket

Frontage Rd.

Clinton

Natchez

W. College St.

Clinton   Blvd

Motels

Raymond- Clinton

Rd.

US 80

Spring Ridge Rd.

I-20

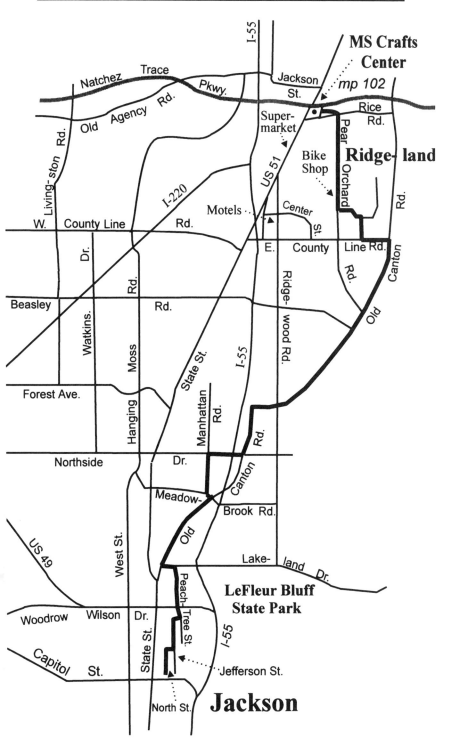

JACKSON TO JEFF BUSBY
mp 102-193

Highlights: Brashear's Stand, Reservoir Overlook, Boyd Mounds, West Florida Boundary, Cypress Swamp, Upper Choctaw Boundary, Robinson Road, Red Dog Road, Myrick Creek, Kosciusko, Hurricane Creek, Cole Creek, Bethel Mission, French Camp, Jeff Busby.

Terrain: Flat-to-rolling near Jackson, becoming rolling further north with a few hills near Jeff Busby.

Northbound Elevation: 300 ft. difference; 1,600 accumulated; 18 ft. average per mile.

Southbound Elevation: 300 ft. difference; 1,500 accumulated; 16 ft. average per mile.

Camping: Timbelake (mp 104), Ratliff Ferry (mp 123), Kosciusko (mp 160), French Camp (mp 181), Jeff Busby (mp 193).

Lodging: Canton (mp 115), Kosciusko (mp 160), French Camp (mp 181).

Without the scenic hills and valleys found near Natchez and north of Tupelo, the miles and miles of trees and grass along this portion of the Trace can get monotonous. Although there is plenty of rural scenery on which to feast the eyes, many more interesting experiences await cyclists who occasionally get off their bikes. By strolling the grounds at French Camp, pedaling into Kosciusko, or walking a peaceful nature trail through a dark bottomland forest, you'll find that touring on two wheels provides opportunities to engage the mind, the senses, and, of course, your legs.

While this may be the flattest portion of the Parkway, the terrain will still make you shift frequently, and a few hills near Jeff Busby are guaranteed to raise your heart rate. Just north of Ridgeland, the Parkway follows eight miles of shoreline along Ross Barnett Reservoir which is part of the Pearl River. The breezes along this lake are always welcome in the summertime (even when they are headwinds!).

The original Trace followed a ridge dividing the Pearl River flowing to the Gulf and the Big Black River which joins the Mississippi River. Before settlement, much of the land near these rivers was impenetrable swamps or soggy bottomland forest. Although teaming with wildlife, it was not ideal for people, horses, or wagons. So for 150 miles, the Trace dodged the worst terrain by staying on this ridge. A short walk on the nature trails at **Myrick Creek**, **Hurricane Creek**, and **Cole Creek** gives us a glimpse of how the Mississippi wilderness appeared with countless acres of cypress-tupelo swamps and hardwood bottomlands that disappeared as the land was drained for cultivation.

The **Cypress Swamp** just north of the reservoir is a popular spot along the Parkway. Visitors can stroll along the boardwalk while viewing these fascinating cypress trees with their knobby "knees" sticking out of the murky water. It also offers a chance possibly to witness an alligator at the northernmost edge of their territory. I was awed by the beauty of this place at dawn on a misty summer morning.

Cypress Swamp

In contrast to the foreboding swamps, **Kosciusko** offers travelers a taste of southern hospitality in small town Mississippi. Be sure to stop at the visitor center which was built by donations and is staffed by volunteers. The town is named after Tadeuz Kosciuszko, a Polish engineer and military officer who came to North America to serve George Washington during the Revolution. He was responsible for designing key fortifications including West Point on the Hudson River. Later he became enraged at the practice of slavery in the South and left money in his will to free slaves. The executor of the will, Thomas Jefferson, himself a slave owner, never carried out Kosciusko's wishes.

After the Treaty of Dancing Rabbit Creek in the 1830s, the town was founded at the site of Redbud Springs, a water stop on the Natchez Trace. Today, the town is known as the birthplace of talk show host Oprah Winfrey who lived here until she was six years old.

There certainly isn't a lack of accommodations in Kosciusko with several restaurants, antique stores, and a bed & breakfast near the town square surrounding the stately 1897 courthouse. If you aren't willing to make the two-mile ride to the town square, three motels, a pizza place, Mexican restaurant, and a Southern style "meat n' three" are adjacent to the Parkway. This is also the best grocery stop and the only laundry stop between Jackson and Tupelo.

After cycling through pine and hardwood forests near milepost 180, you come to a large clearing dotted with trees. These are the grounds of the **French Camp Academy**. The name comes from the stand built in 1812 by Frenchman Louis LeFleur. He also established a trading post called LeFleur's Bluff that later became Jackson. His half-Indian son, Greenwood, became the last Choctaw chief of this district and played an important role in negotiating the Treaty of Dancing Rabbit Creek with Andrew Jackson. This treaty called for the final removal of the Choctaw to Oklahoma, but allowed those who agreed to live under U.S. law to remain with 640 acres of land per family. Greenwood was later elected to the state senate and became an affluent plantation owner near present day Greenwood, Mississippi.

In 1885, a group of Scot-Irish immigrants founded the French Camp Academy as a boarding school for boys. Today, this coed facility is a not-for-profit boarding school for children "in need of a stable home environment where they are loved and wanted." Besides a rigorous academic program, students are exposed to a curriculum ranging from farming to computer skills.

The restored 1846 Drane House immediately greets visitors as they walk onto the academy grounds from the Parkway. Here you will find rooms furnished with period

Drane House at French Camp

furniture, and you might, as we did, observe school girls being taught the art of quilting. The Huffman Log Cabin (1840) was relocated to this site and currently houses a gift shop and restaurant. You may purchase their homemade sorghum molasses which is made on the grounds during the Fall Festival in October. (They ship so you don't have to carry it on your bike.) This log cabin restaurant (open 10:30 a.m.- 2:30 p.m.) is locally famous for its potato soup, plus their homemade bread is equally delicious. The French Camp Bed & Breakfast has hosted countless cyclists.

Nestled in the Red Clay Hills, you'll find the **Jeff Busby** site, named in honor of the Mississippi congressmen who sponsored legislation to establish the Parkway. Here you will find a campground, picnic area, and nature trails. A 1-mile spur road with a surprisingly challenging 200 ft. climb leads to the top of Little Mountain (603 ft.) with sweeping views in several directions. If you have more time, a shaded hiking trail will also take you to the top.

While camping here, I met a couple from Colorado who quit their jobs, sold the house, went backpacking for two months, rode their tandem from Colorado to Texas and were continuing to Washington, D.C. After that they planned to go sea kayaking along the Southeastern coast. You have to admire such a spirit of adventure!

Milepost

102.4   US 51/Parkway Information Center (**W, RR, Visitors Center, PS, Rst, Supermkt, Ldg, Bike Shop**). See *Jackson Section.* Northbound cyclists may use the **paved multi-use trail** (see mp 105.6).

103.4   Madison/Old Canton Rd. (**Cpg**). Timberlake Campground (private 601/992-9100 or 877/388-2267 (showers) is 4.5 miles east of the Parkway along the lake. Follow the bike path along Old Canton Rd. and then turn left on Lake

Harbour Dr. which becomes Spillway Rd. A supermarket and restaurants are on the route.

104.5   Brashear's Stand/Mississippi Crafts Center. Advertised as a "house of entertainment in the wilderness," nothing remains of this inn except for the sunken trace, now a nature trail, that brought countless travelers to this stand. A short trail leads to the Mississippi Crafts Center which is adjacent to the Parkway.

105.6   Reservoir Overlook/Mutli-use Trail. (access to **Mkt, Rst, Supermkt, Bike Shop**). A grassy hill provides views of Ross Barnett Reservoir, a man-made lake on the Pearl River. A paved multi-use trail (still under construction in 2009) heads south along the parkway for 5 miles allowing cyclists to escape this often busy segment of the Trace. The spur path along Pear Orchard Rd. connects up with small markets, restaurants, and a bike shop. The other spur along Old Canton Rd. leads to a supermarket within one mile. Both spurs head south (or east) of the Parkway).

106.9   Boyd Mounds. This Woodland period mound is actually three mounds joined together measuring a total length of 100 ft. This mound was used for several centuries.

107.9   West Florida Boundary. This boundary was established after Great Britain gained control following the French and Indian War of 1763.

114.9   MS 43 (**Ldg**). Heart's Content B&B $$-$$$ (601/859-0109) is located 8 miles away in Canton. Shuttle service available.

122.0   Cypress Swamp. A beautiful cypress-tupelo swamp is visible from the parking area. A boardwalk leads across the swamp where a dirt path follows its edge.

122.6   River Bend (**W, RR**). This shaded picnic area is located on the Pearl River.

123.7   Ratliff Ferry (**Mkt, Cpg**). This private campground (showers)(601/859-1810) is on the reservoir .5

mi. east of the Parkway. Also has a market with a fair selection of non-perishable food.

128.4 Upper Choctaw Boundary. In 1820 Andrew Jackson signed a treaty with Choctaw Indians at Doak's Stand on the old Natchez Trace. The Choctaws ceded one-third of their land, nearly 5.5 million acres.

135.0 MS 16/Canton (**Mkt, Rst**). A market and restaurant are 1.5 mi. west toward Canton.

135.5 Robinson Road. Built in 1821 between Columbus and Jackson, this road became the mail route causing further decline of the Natchez Trace.

140.0 Red Dog Road. This road running to Canton was built in 1834 and named after a Choctaw Chief who had become a farmer accepting the ways of his new neighbors.

145.1 Myrick Creek is a nature trail about beavers who are no longer there. The beavers left after the park service put up signs explaining the ways of this bucktooth critter. They can be seen elsewhere along the Parkway and who knows, maybe they'll be back.

146.2 MS 429/Thomastown (**Mkt, Rst**). A market and restaurant are .5 mi. west of the Parkway.

154.3 Holly Hill Picnic Area (**W, RR, PS**).

160.0 MS 35/Kosciusko (**W, RR, Visitor Center, Supermkt, Rst, Ldg, Cpg, Laundry**). The visitor center which is adjacent to the Parkway provides a free street map including the location of various services. To reach the historic downtown, take MS 19/Huntington St. which is across MS 35 from the NTP access road. In 2 miles you will see the courthouse/town square to the left. See listing on p. 77 for restaurants. A coin laundry and mid-size supermarket are along Huntington St. The Maple Terrace B&B $$-$$$ (662/289-5353) is located near the square. An Americas Best Value Inn $$ (662/289-6252 or 888/315-2378), Days Inn $-$$ (662/289-2271 or 800/DAYSINN), and Super 8 $$ (662/289-7880 or 800/800/8000) are located on MS 35 within view of the Parkway.

A SuperWalmart (supermarket) is one mile west on MS 35. A bicyclists-only campground (no showers) is located in a wooded area along the access road to the Park Service maintenance area just south of MS 35. It is to the right just before the gate to the maintenance yard. Contact www.kadcorp.org or 662/289-2981 for more tourist info.

164.3 Hurricane Creek. A nature trail winds through a variety of vegetation from wet bottomland along Hurricane Creek to the top of a dry hill.

175.6 Cole Creek. The cypress-tupelo swamp along this creek is being slowly replaced with a bottomland forest consisting of beech, hickory, red oak, chestnut oak, ash, and elm.

176.3 Bethel Mission. A Choctaw mission operated near here from 1822-1826. The missionaries also taught farming, carpentry, weaving, and housekeeping as well as reading and arithmetic.

180.7 French Camp (**W, RR, Mkt, Rst, Cpg, Ldg**). This not-for-profit boarding school has restored two historic homes which are open to visitors. The Council House Cafe is open from 10:30-2:30 Mon.- Sat., and other meals may be available at the school cafeteria with prior arrangement. There is also a bakery. The French Camp Academy B&B $$ (662/547-6835) is also located on the campus. Camping and hostel-style lodging may be available with advance arrangements. Call 662/547-9464 for general information. A market well-stocked with non-perishable groceries is across the Parkway.

193.1 Jeff Busby (**W, RR, Cpg**). The campground (no showers) and picnic area are within a half mile of the Parkway. This site also features a steep one-mile spur road climbing 200 ft. in elevation to the top of Little Mountain (603 ft.).

JEFF BUSBY TO TUPELO
mp 193-266

Highlights: Pigeon Roost, Line Creek, Bynum Mounds, Witch Dance, Chickasaw Agency, Owl Creek Mounds, Hernando de Soto, Monroe Mission, Tockshish, Chickasaw Council House, Black Belt Overlook, Chickasaw Village, Old Town Overlook, Tupelo Visitor Center.

Terrain: Flat-to-rolling. Climbs are either short, or the grades are very gradual.

Northbound Elevation: 250 ft. difference; 1,680 ft. accumulated; 23 ft. average per mile.

Southbound Elevation: 250 ft. difference; 1,830 ft. accumulated; 25 ft. average per mile.

Camping: Red Hills RV Park (mp 195.3), Witch Dance (mp 233), Davis Lake (mp 243), Natchez Trace RV Complex (mp 252), Natchez Trace Visitor Center (mp 266).

Lodging: US 82 in Mathiston (mp 204), MS 8 in Houston (mp 229), Natchez Trace RV Complex (mp 252), MS 6 in Tupelo (mp 260), Barnes Crossing (mp 266).

We can only imagine what this part of Mississippi looked like when Spaniard **Hernando de Soto** led a three year expedition on foot and horseback from Florida to Arkansas. Approximately 1,000 *conquistadors* spent the winter among the Chickasaw Indians of this area until the Chickasaws attacked in March of 1541. De Soto and his men fled west to become the first known Europeans to step foot on the Indian trail later known as the Natchez Trace *and* to lay eyes on the Mississippi River.

It took De Soto three months to reach the Mississippi near Memphis from the Natchez Trace, a distance that could be cycled in a few days—pavement has its advantages! This holds true while pedaling the central section of the Natchez Trace where the miles fly by with only minor hills and few distractions. The vast hardwood-pine forests that once towered over the De Soto Expedition have all disappeared, but miles of mature second growth trees line the Parkway today. The virgin forests were cleared for cotton, a crop that ruled the region's economy for many years. Today, timber is king, but several cotton fields and pastures, symbolic of the rural South, can be seen while you cycle the Trace.

Going north from Jeff Busby, the Trace rolls up and down the Red Clay Hills before settling into the bottomlands near the headwaters of the Big Black River. One of its tributaries, **Line Creek**, served as a dividing line between the Chickasaw and Choctaw Nations. The legends of these people tell of their forefathers coming here from the west. In the hills of origin known as "Nanih Waiya," these people separated, becoming enemies who were often at war. The exhibit at the **Bynum Mounds** explains how the earlier inhabitants of the Woodland period had already established a trade network from the Great Lakes to the Gulf Coast.

The rest area at **Witch Dance** tells us a very different story, one of local witches who used to gather here and dance, causing the grass to wither and die wherever their feet touched. Today equestrian, hikers, and mountain bikers gather in the cooler months to enjoy the trails through the Tombigbee National Forest. Bicyclist and equestrian camping is permitted but should you hear dancing and laughter at night, I suggest you stay in the tent!

Davis Lake makes a nice lunch detour or camping location with the day use area and campground adjacent to the tranquil lake. I particularly enjoyed swimming here at night under a hazy summer moon with the lightning bugs blinking overhead.

Nearing Tupelo, the Trace traverses the cultivated bottomlands of the **Tombigbee Prairie**. Chiwapa and Coonewah Creeks have been straightened and diked, draining the acres of difficult wetlands the Kaintucks once trudged through.

Large sections of this area were originally grass prairie where numerous bison, bears, and wolves foraged for food.

Tupelo offers cyclists all the amenities of civilization only a short distance from the Trace. The *Tupelo Tour* (p. 87) provides a pleasant change of pace with an interesting excursion to the historic downtown and the Elvis Presley Birthplace. Numerous opportunities for lodging and dining are available along this route that bypasses six miles of the Parkway.

Bovine scenery in central Mississippi

Milepost

195.3   MS 9 (**Mkt**). A market reasonably stocked with non-perishable goods is .1 mi. east of the Parkway.

201.3   Ballard Creek Picnic Area

203.5   Pigeon Roost. Folsom Stand and Trading Post was located in these woods along Pigeon Roost Creek where millions of passenger pigeons, now extinct, once roosted. The Trading Post, operated by Nathaniel Folsom and his Choctaw wife, was in business by 1790.

204.2   US 82/Mathiston (**Mkt, Supermkt, Rst, Ldg**). Use the southern exit to access US 82 East. A market (snacks and drinks) and restaurant are .5 mi. east of the Parkway, and a supermarket is 1.5 mi. east on US 82 and MS 15 South. The Mathiston Motel $ (662/263-8219) is .8 mi. east of the Parkway.

213.3   Line Creek. This creek, now channeled, formed the boundary between the Choctaw Nation to the south and the Chickasaw Nation to the north. Noah Wall and his Choctaw wife operated a stand near here.

219.5   MS 46/Mantee (**Mkt, Rst**). A market (drinks and snacks) is .2 mi. west of the Trace. Also serves BBQ and pizza for lunch.

229.5   MS 8/Houston (**Mkt, Rst, Ldg**). Restaurants and a supermarket are 4 mi. west in the town of Houston. Bridges Hall Manor B&B $$ (662/456-4071), the Holiday Terrace Motel $ (662/456-2522), and Western Inn and Suites $-$$ (662/456-4222) are also located in Houston.

232.4   Bynum Mounds. Two 10 ft. mounds remain of the original six burial mounds of this Woodland period site.

233.2   Witch Dance (**W, RR, Cpg**). This shaded picnic area is the trailhead for horse trails in the Tombigbee National Forest. Mountain bikers also use these trails. Camping for bicyclists and equestrians is permitted at the south end of the picnic area.

241.4   Chickasaw Agency. U.S. agents lived along the Old Trace near here from 1802-1825. They had the nearly impossible task of preserving harmony between the Indians and the traveling Kaintucks.

243.2   Davis Lake & Owl Creek Mounds (**Cpg**). Davis Lake Recreation Area (day use and camping fee) is 4 mi. west of the Trace on CR 124. This area features a swim area, picnic shelters, and fishing in addition to the campground with showers. Owl Creek Mound, consisting of two mounds, is located 3 mi. from the Trace en route to Davis Lake.

243.3   Hernando de Soto. In 1540, 261 years before the U.S. Government designated the Natchez Trace as a national road, Spanish explorer Hernando de Soto crossed the Trace near this location.

245.6   Monroe Mission. Beginning in 1822, Chickasaws were taught Christianity and various skills of western civilization.

249.6   Tockshish. This community of Indians and white men was established by British agent John McIntosh prior to 1770. In 1801, it became a post office where postriders would exchange horses during the 12 day journey between Nashville and Natchez.

251.1   Chickasaw Council House. The village of Pontotoc, capital of the Chickasaw Nation, was located west of here on the original Natchez Trace. Each summer two to three thousand Indians would camp nearby to collect payments for lands ceded to the U.S. A town and county in Oklahoma are named after the original capital of the Chickasaw Nation.

251.6   Pontocola Rd./CR 506 (**Mkt, Rst, Ldg, Cpg, Laundry**). A market well-stocked with non-perishable groceries is .3 mi. west of the Parkway. The Natchez Trace RV Complex (private, 662/767-8609) (showers, laundry) is located .4 mi. off the Trace to the east. Cabins are also available in addition to tent sites. The adjacent restaurant is open for dinner only.

255.1   Palmetto Rd. (**Mkt**). A market well-stocked with non-perishable goods is .9 mi. east of the Parkway.

255.3   Black Belt Overlook. This valley along Chiwapa Creek is part of the Black Belt or Black Prairie extending from Columbus, MS into Alabama. The black soil supported a vast prairie grassland which the settlers cultivated into a leading cotton producing area. Today, this area is mostly pastureland.

260.0   MS 6/Main St. - Tupelo (**Supermkt, Rst, Ldg, Bike Shop, Laundry**). A large supermarket, Walmart, and fast food establishments are .8 mi. east on Main St. A convenience store and restaurant are .3 mi. off the Trace to the west. See *Tupelo Tour* (p. 87) for additional services.

261.8   Chickasaw Village

262.3   McCullough Blvd./MS 178 (**Rst, Ldg, Bike Shop**). Several motels, restaurants, and Trails & Treads (662/690-6620) are located 2 mi. east (busy highway) at the intersection of North Gloster St. See *Tupelo Tour* for lodging info.

263.9   Old Town Overlook

266.0   Natchez Trace Headquarters/Visitor Center (**W, RR, Supermkt, Rst, Ldg, Cpg**). The Visitor Center displays several artifacts, photos, and drawings of the natural and human history along the Natchez Trace. Barnes Crossing, 1.5 mi. away, has an Americas Best Value Inn $$ (662/842-4403), a large supermarket, and restaurants (follow *Tupelo Tour* southbound, p. 91). An unmarked bicyclist campground (no showers) with picnic tables, screened-in cabins (not bug proof), and water is located just west of the Parkway. Take the access road across the Parkway from the Visitor Center (directly opposite mp 266). In .15 mi., look for a trailhead parking area on the left of this road. Across the road from this parking area is a barricaded gravel trail. A 5 minute walk on this trail leads to the camping area.

THE TUPELO TOUR

Highlights: Tupelo Museum, Tupelo National Battle-
field, Tupelo Hardware, Courthouse and Square,
Elvis Presley Birthplace, Elvis Presley Lake.
Terrain: Mostly flat.
Camping: Natchez Trace Parkway Visitor Center (see
p. 86).
Lodging: The nearest motel to the Trace is at Barnes
Crossing which 1.5 miles from the Parkway Visitor
Center. Several motels closer to downtown are on
or near the Tupelo Tour.

Tupelo, the "smallest big city" along the Trace, offers
all the amenities of civilization in a small town atmosphere.
The *Tupelo Tour* takes you into the heart of town before
returning to the Trace six miles from where you exited,
adding 7 miles to your journey. Day riders can pedal a
pleasant 20-mile loop by beginning at the Parkway Visitor
Center and returning northbound on the Parkway. Although
a few short busy stretches are unavoidable, street-wise cyclists should feel comfortable on these roads also utilized by
the local riders heading out to the country. Of course this
urban excursion will be more enjoyable if you avoid commuting hours.

After the Chickasaws vacated this area following the
Treaty of Pontotoc in 1832, the town of Harrisburg was
founded. When the railroad tracks were laid just to the east
in a grove of Tupelo Gum trees, the population soon relocated by the tracks and later renamed itself to honor the trees
used to build their new community.

The edge of town became a deadly battlefield during
the **Battle of Tupelo** as General Nathan Bedford Forrest's
10,000 troops attacked the 14,000 Union troops of General

A.J. Smith. Although the Union withdrew, the Confederates sustained heavy losses and never succeeded in their quest to cut the Union's railroad supply line.

Tupelo's big fortune came in 1887 when the Memphis and Birmingham Railroad crossed the existing Mobile and Ohio tracks in town. Business boomed, and the population quickly grew. In 1935, another important event occurred, but no one knew it—the King was born! In a modest two-room house, **Elvis Presley** grew up in Tupelo and purchased his first guitar at the Tupelo Hardware Store (still in business) on Main St. His birthplace and an adjacent museum are conveniently located along the *Tupelo Tour* for all the cycling Elvis fans.

The Tupelo City Museum (admission only $1), just west of the Trace on Main St./MS 6, contains a surprising variety of items ranging from Elvis memorabilia to Chickasaw dwellings and artifacts. The space hangar displays moon rocks and space equipment. From the Parkway, a gated gravel road (at mp 259.2—just south of Main St.) provides easy access for cyclists desiring to visit the museum.

Elvis Presley Birthplace

Many of the locally owned eateries are closed on Sundays but the chain restaurants will be glad to serve you. Call the Visitor Bureau (662/841-6521 or 800/533-0611) or visit www.tupelo.net for information on lodging, dining, and attractions plus a free street map. You may also stop by the Tupelo Visitor Center located at the Arena at 399 East Main St.

Downtown Restaurants

Barb-B-Q by Jim—Commerce St.—one block east of Spring St. (Mon.-Wed. 11-6; Thur.-Sat. 11-?) Casual barbecue place.

Cancun Mexican Restaurant—N. Gloster just north of Main St. and also at Barnes Crossing on Tupelo Tour (lunch and dinner) Menu varies from fajitas to healthy light items.

Harvey's—424 S. Gloster (Mon.-Sat. lunch and dinner) Sandwiches, steaks, seafood, and pasta.

Stables Bar and Grill—N. Spring St. Alley (Mon.-Sat. 10 a.m. midnight) Plate lunches, steak & seafood with a southern flair.

Tupelo Tour (Northbound)

Mile

0.0   At mp 259.8, exit the Parkway using the first exit for Main St./MS 6 (**Mkt, Rst**). Use the second exit to access the Tupelo City Museum.

0.3   **Right** at the end of the access ramp onto Main St./MS 6 going east toward town.

0.8   **Left** on Thomas St. at the traffic light. (**Supermkt, Rst**). A SuperWalmart with groceries is located .5 mi. toward town on Main St.)

1.5   **Right** on Jackson St. at the traffic light (**Bike Shop**). Bicycle Pacelines (662/844-8660) is .5 mi. to the left on Jackson St.

2.0   Cross Lumpkin Ave. (**Laundry**).

3.2   Cross N. Gloster St. at the traffic light (**Rst, Ldg**). The Scottish Inn $ (bicycle discount)(662/842-1961) is within .5 mi. to the left (north) on N. Gloster St. The Days Inn $-$$ (662-842-0088 or 800/DAYSINN), Economy Inn $ (662/842-1213), Travelodge $$ (662/844-4111 or 800/578-7878), Howard Johnson Express $$ (662/842-8811 or 800/LGOHOJO) and restaurants are within one mile to the left (north) on N. Gloster St. (This is a busy 4-lane highway.)

3.9   **Right** on N. Broadway at the water tower.

4.4   **Left** on Main St./MS 6 just past the courthouse (**Rst**). Several restaurants (see restaurant listing) are located near the courthouse.

4.7   Tupelo Visitor Bureau (**Ldg**). Hilton Garden $$-$$$ (662/718-5500 or 877/STAYHGI)

5.2   Go under US 45 (**Mkt, Rst, Ldg**). Americas Best Value Inn $ (662/844-8456)

5.8   **Left** on Elvis Presley Dr. Elvis Presley Birthplace and Museum.

6.0   **Right**, staying on Elvis Presley Dr. just past his birthplace (stop sign).

6.3   Veterans Park (**W, RR, PS**).

8.0	**Left** on Oakview Dr. (4-way stop).
8.2	**Right** on N. Veterans Blvd. (stop sign at the T-intersection)(**Rst**).
8.5	Go under US 78 (**Mkt**). Road becomes CR 811.
8.7	Cross CR 1460 (**Mkt**).
10.9	**Left** on Barnes Crossing Rd./CR 843 (stop sign).
12.2	Cross N. Gloster St. (traffic light) and immediately go **right** on Beech Springs Rd./CR 681 (**Supermkt, Rst, Ldg**). Americas Best Value Inn $$ (662/842-4403 or 800/528-1234).
13.4	**Right** on access road after going under the NTP.
13.7	Natchez Trace Parkway Visitor Center (**W, RR, Cpg**). See p. 86 for directions to cyclists-only campground.

Tupelo Tour (Southbound)

Mile

0.0	Go west on the access road directly across from mp 266 at the Parkway Visitor Center.
0.3	**Left** on CR 681/Beech Springs Rd. (stop sign at the T-intersection).
1.4	**Left** at the stop sign and immediately cross N. Gloster St./MS 145 at the traffic light. (**Supermkt, Rst, Ldg**). Best Western Motel $$ (662/842-4403 or 800/528-1234).
2.7	**Right** on CR 811 (stop sign at the 4-way intersection) (**Rst**).
4.9	Cross CR 1460 (**Mkt**).
5.1	Road becomes N. Veterans Blvd. as you go under US 78 (**Mkt**).
5.4	**Left** on Oakview Dr. (first left after going under US 78.) (**Rst**).
5.5	**Right** on Elvis Presley Dr. (4-way stop).
7.2	Veterans Park (**W, RR, PS**).
7.4	**Left**, staying on Elvis Presley Dr., where Reese St. goes straight (stop sign). Elvis Presley Birthplace and Museum.

7.6   **Right** on Main St./MS 6. (traffic light).
8.4   Go under US 45 (**Mkt, Rst, Ldg**). Americas Best Value Inn $ (662/844-8456)
8.7   Tupelo Visitor Bureau (**Ldg**). Hilton Garden $$-$$$ (662/718-5500 or 877/STAYHGI)
9.0   **Right** on N. Spring St. (traffic light)(**Rst**) in the historic downtown area. See restaurant listings.
9.1   **Left** on Jefferson St. (traffic light).
9.2   **Right** on Broadway (traffic light).
9.6   **Left** on Jackson St. (stop sign).
10.1 Cross N. Gloster St. at the traffic light (**Rst, Ldg**). The Scottish Inn $ (bicycle discount)(662/842-1961) is within .5 mi. to the right (north) on N. Gloster St. The Days Inn $-$$ (662-842-0088 or 800/DAYSINN) Economy Inn $ (662/842-1213), Travelodge $$ (662/844-4111 or 800/578-7878), Howard Johnson Express $$ (601/842-8811 OR 800/LGOHOJO) and restaurants are within one mile to the right (north) on N. Gloster St. (busy 4-lane highway.)
11.4 Cross Lumpkin Ave. (**Laundry**).
11.9 **Left** on Thomas St. at the traffic light (**Bike Shop**). Bicycle Pacelines (662/844-8660) is .5 mi. straight ahead on Jackson St.
12.6 **Right** on W. Main/MS 6 at the traffic light (**Supermkt, Rst**). A SuperWalmart with groceries is .5 mi. east (to the left) on Main St.
13.3 **Right** on Natchez Trace Parkway (**Mkt, Rst**). The Tupelo City Museum lies just west of the Parkway.

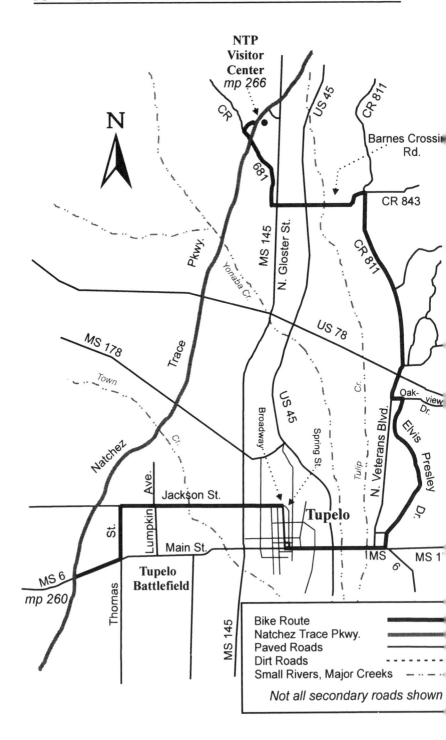

NTP Visitor Center
mp 266

N

CR

US 45

CR 811

Barnes Crossi
Rd.

681

CR 843

MS 145

N. Gloster St.

CR 811

Pkwy.

Yonaba Cr.

US 78

MS 178

Trace

Town

US 45

Broadway

Spring St.

Tulip Cr.

Oak- view
Dr.

N. Veterans Blvd.

Elvis

Natchez

Cr.

Presley

Ave.

Jackson St.

Lumpkin

Tupelo

Dr.

St.

Main St.

MS 6

MS 1

MS 6
mp 260

**Tupelo
Battlefield**

Thomas

MS 145

Bike Route	▬▬▬
Natchez Trace Pkwy.	▬▬▬
Paved Roads	────
Dirt Roads	- - - -
Small Rivers, Major Creeks	─ ·· ─ ·· ─

Not all secondary roads shown

TUPELO VISITOR CENTER
TO COLBERT FERRY
mp 266-327

Highlights: Confederate Graves, Dogwood Valley, Twentymile Bottom Overlook, Donivan Slough, Pharr Mounds, Tennessee-Tombigbee Waterway, Tishomingo State Park, Cave Spring, Bear Creek Mound, Mississippi/Alabama Line, Freedom Hills Overlook, Buzzard Roost Spring, Colbert Ferry.

Terrain:, Mostly gentle rolling hills near Tupelo. Moderate to challenging hills between the Tenn-Tom Waterway and Colbert Ferry.

Northbound Elevation: 440 ft. difference; 1,550 ft. accumulated; 25 ft. average per mile.

Southbound Elevation: 440 ft. difference; 1,400 ft. accumulated; 23 ft. average per mile.

Camping: Whip-Poor-Will (mp 293), Tishomingo State Park (mp 303), Colbert Ferry (mp 327).

Lodging: MS 370 in Baldwyn (mp 280) (12 miles off parkway, shuttle available), Belmont and Tishomingo State Park (mp 302).

From the prairie to the mountains, this portion of the Parkway takes you through a variety of terrain varying from the wetlands of the Tombigbee Prairie to the foothills of the Appalachian Mountains. The difference isn't as dramatic as what you would experience in Colorado, but the observant cyclist is bound to notice the botanical and geological difference. For those not so observant, your legs will surely let you know!

North of Tupelo, the Trace drops down to **Twentymile Bottom**, a strip of fertile farmland drained by canals. In the early days, these bottomlands produced nothing but misery for the weary travelers. In 1812 Reverend John Johnson passed through this area and wrote this account of his journey: "I have this day swam my horse five times, bridged one creek, forded several others beside the swamp we had to wade through. At night we had a shower of rain. Took up my usual lodging on the ground in company with several Indians."

A short walk through **Donivan Slough** gives a glimpse of what these vast bottomlands must have been like. Elevation differences of only a few feet determine what type of plant life will thrive. Tulip Poplar, Sycamore, River Birch, and Water Oak grow on the higher ground that occasionally floods, while Tupelo and Bald Cypress grow only in the wet slough.

Heading north, the Trace travels over gently rolling hills covered with thick forests before reaching a large wooded wetland adjacent to the **Tennessee-Tombigbee Waterway**. In the 1770s, French explorer Sieur de Bienville recommended to Louis XIV that a canal be built connecting these two rivers. In 1985, the U.S. Army Corp of Engineers completed the job. The waterway provides a 450-mile passage for barges and shallow draft boats from the Tennessee River to the Gulf of Mexico. At ten times over budget, the waterway cost taxpayers $1.8 billion to complete plus $19 million a year to maintain.

While many hail it as an economic boon, the waterway receives only one quarter of the predicted traffic. The Tenn-Tom Waterway does provide recreational opportunities (including mountain biking along the canal) and a habitat for birds and other wildlife. While mountain biking on a hot summer day, we observed herons, egrets, kingfishers, and wild turkey. A pair of bald eagles also resides nearby. Recently, beavers constructed a large dam by the parking area adjacent to the Tenn-Tom Waterway.

North of the waterway, the Trace heads for the hills going from 360 feet in elevation to almost 800 feet at the **Freedom Hills** overlook in Alabama. While pedaling these hills (it is hilly both ways), notice the sandstone rock formations and the twisting valley carved by Bear Creek. This region is the southwestern most extension of the Appalachians, or more precisely, the tip of the western ridge known as the Cumberland Plateau. Although this does not match the grandeur of the Blue Ridge Parkway, you will get a taste of Appalachian plants and geology. By cycling into **Tishomingo State Park**, you will discover a boulder-strewn landscape in a forested setting. It is 3.5 miles one-way to the swinging bridge over Bear Creek. A trail twisting through large rock formations is located one mile from the Parkway.

Another interesting geologic feature is **Cave Springs**, a very welcomed location because the 60 degree temperatures at the mouth of this cave provide a comforting refuge from the summer heat.

Remnants of the Native Americans are evident in names like Tishomingo, a Chickasaw chief (1750-1836) who hunted in the Freedom Hills with his tribesmen. George Colbert, the half Scot-half Chickasaw chief operated a stand and **Colbert Ferry** across the Tennessee River until 1820. He is reputed to have once charged Andrew Jackson $75,000 to ferry his army across the river, an example of early price-gouging by defense contractors!

Bear Creek in Alabama

While very little remains of the proud Chickasaw Nation in Mississippi, evidence of the mound builders can be seen at two sites. **Pharr Mounds**, consisting of eight dome shaped mounds, is the most significant archaeological site in northern Mississippi. Many artifacts have been retrieved from this site spanning the mid-Woodland to Mississippian era (100-1200 A.D.). These nomadic tribes would return here for ceremonies and to bury their dead. The **Bear Creek Mound** is the oldest prehistoric site along the Trace and was probably occupied for several thousand years, from Paleo all the way to Mississippian (8000 B.C.-1000 A.D.).

Milepost

269.4	Confederate Gravesites. A short walk on a sunken portion of the Old Trace leads to the unmarked graves of 13 Confederate soldiers.
270.7	MS 363 (**Mkt, Rst, Supermkt, Laundry**). A market with a few non-perishable goods is .7 mi. west toward Saltillo. A small supermarket, restaurant, and laundry are 1.5 mi. west in Saltillo
275.2	Dogwood Valley. A nature trail leads through a grove of Dogwood Trees that bloom a pleasing soft-white in April.
278.4	Twentymile Bottom Overlook. A view of the cultivated bottomlands.
280.1	MS 370/Baldwyn (**Mkt, Ldg**). Sachem B&B $$ (662/346-3652) will shuttle cyclists to Baldwyn which is 12 miles west of the Parkway. A market is 1.5 miles east on MS 371 toward Mantachie.
283.3	Donivan Slough. A short trail takes you through a mature bottomland forest.
286.7	Pharr Mounds (**W, RR, PS**). The eight mounds located on this 90-acre grassy plain were built nearly 2,000 years ago.
293.2	Tennessee-Tombigbee Waterway. A picnic area is adjacent to the waterway and within view of Bay Springs Lock and Dam.

293.5   CR 1/Bay Springs Lake (**Cpg**). Whip-Poor-Will Campground (private, 662/728-2449, showers) is located 3 mi. away at the Bay Springs Marina. Go 1 mi. north on CR 1 (toward the dam), then left on MS 4 for1.5 mi. Turn right at the West Damside Recreation Area and follow the signs to the marina. There is a small market (snacks) and cabins (no bedding or cooking utensils) at Whip-Poor-Will Campground. Another market with a fair selection of can goods and meats is .5 mi. away.

296.0   Jourdon Creek Picnic Area

302.0   MS 25 (**Mkt, Rst, Ldg**). A market with a few non-perishable goods and a restaurant open Thur.-Sat. are .5 mi. west of the Parkway. You can enter Tishomingo State Park from the road directly across MS 25 from the market. The Belmont Hotel B&B $ (662/454-7948 or 888/826-6023) is located 6 miles east on MS 25. Restaurants and a small supermarket can also be found in the town of Belmont.

302.8   Tishomingo State Park (**Cpg, Ldg**) (662/438-6914). This state park, with Appalachian-like geology and mature hardwood forests, offers hiking, canoeing, swimming, fishing, and a suspension bridge over Bear Creek. Go west on the access road and turn right at the T-intersection (a small market is 1.3 mi. to the left). The campground (which has nearby picnic shelters, showers, and coin laundry) is 1.5 mi. from the Trace. The cabins ($$—may require two night stay) are an additional 2.5 mi. from the campground.

308.4   Cave Springs. This clear cool pool near the cave's mouth was a water source for Indians and Kaintucks.

308.8   Bear Creek Mound. This ceremonial structure was built between 1200 A.D. and 1400 A.D.

308.9   Mississippi-Alabama state line.

313.0   Bear Creek Picnic Area. Shaded tables are located along the large creek. Also canoe access.

317.0   Freedom Hills Overlook. A short uphill trail leads to an overlook at 800 ft.—the highest elevation on the Parkway in Alabama.

320.3   Buzzard Roost Spring/US 72 (**Mkt, Supermkt, Rst**). Chickasaw Chief Levi Colbert operated a stand near this spring which can be reached by a short shaded trail. A market (mostly snacks) is located 1.3 mi. off the Parkway by going east on US 72. A supermarket and restaurant are an additional mile east in Cherokee. The Wooden Nickel, a popular home-style eatery, is located on the tiny Main St.

326.1   CR 21. This county road can be used to create a detour through Cherokee (**Mkt, Supermkt, Rst**—see above) that joins the Parkway at US 72 (see *Cherokee Loop* on p. 182 for directions).

327.3   Colbert Ferry (**W, RR, PS, Cpg**). Chickasaw Chief George Colbert operated a ferry across the Tennessee River. A small visitor center is located just off the Parkway, and a picnic area on Pickwick Lake is a pleasant 3-mile roundtrip. To reach the unsigned bicycle-only camp area from the visitor center, go left toward the picnic area/boat ramp for .1 mi. to where the main road turns right. You will see two gated roads at this turn. Go past the gate that is straight ahead and a few yards later you will see picnic tables and grills on the right. **Last reliable water northbound for 28 miles.**

COLBERT FERRY TO
MERIWETHER LEWIS
mp 327-386

Highlights: Tennessee River, Rock Springs, Cypress Creek, Sunken Trace, McGlamery Stand, Sweetwater Branch, Glenrock Branch, Dogwood Mudhole, Old Trace Drive, Jack's Branch, Napier Mine, Metal Ford/Buffalo River, Meriwether Lewis.

Terrain: Several long gradual climbs south of Old Trace Drive (mp 375) including a very long northbound climb after the Tennessee River. Three back-to-back climbs (150-200 ft.) in either direction between Old Trace Drive and Meriwether Lewis.

Northbound Elevation: 600 ft. difference; 1,950 ft. accumulated; 33 ft. average per mile.

Southbound Elevation: 600 ft. difference; 1,600 accumulated; 27 ft. average per mile.

Camping: Colbert Ferry (mp 327), CR 14 at Brush Creek County Park (mp 332), Laurel Hill (mp 373), Natchez Trace Wilderness Preserve (mp 381), Meriwether Lewis (mp 386).

Lodging: TN 13/Collinwood (mp 355), US 64 (mp 370) 8 miles away in Waynesboro. Natchez Trace Wilderness Preserve (mp 381), TN 20 in Hohenwald (mp 386). Also 15 miles east in Florence via CR 2 CR 14, or AL 157 (mp 329, 322, 344). See *Appendices* for tourist information and the *Florence Loop* (p. 185) for route possibilities.

From the Tennessee River to the Highland Rim, the Natchez Trace travels along wooded ridges and drops into steep hollows carved by clear creeks cascading over rocky streambeds. The scenery is superb, the traffic is light, and there are plenty of opportunities to stroll along a nature trail or splash around in a cool creek.

Just north of Colbert Ferry, the Parkway crosses the **Tennessee River** on a one-mile bridge spanning Pickwick Lake. Created in 1938 when the Tennessee Valley Authority dammed 50 miles of the river, this lake is the second largest lake on the Tennessee River. This river was probably less than a quarter-mile wide when the Kaintucks ferried across on wooden rafts during the early 19th century. A few miles upriver (east) from the bridge, the treacherous Muscle Shoals rumbled for centuries before being silenced by the Tennessee Valley Authority. Before then, only in high water could large steamboats continue upstream. The town of Waterloo, 10 miles downriver, served as an important port where people and goods were transferred to smaller crafts in order to continue upriver.

Along the north bank in 1865, Major General J.H. Wilson assembled the largest cavalry force ever amassed in the western hemisphere. 22,000 troops trained and camped between the little-used Trace and Waterloo. We can only imagine what it must have smelled like... While on the bridge, there is enough room to pull safely off the roadway to admire the bluffs and wooded shoreline of Pickwick Lake. I had the good fortune to watch a large coal barge sail under my feet.

Rock Springs is one of my favorite spots on this portion of the Trace. The spring runs at a constant 59 degrees and feels absolutely heavenly on a hot summer day. A two-

Parkway bridge over Pickwick Lake

minute walk takes you to a four-foot deep pool with large stepping stones. Passing a beaver dam, the nature trail continues to the spring. I was lucky enough to spot one of these cute critters sitting on a log enjoying its lunch.

If you are pedaling north, your speed will suffer due to an almost imperceptible ascent, rising 600 feet over the next 20 miles. Fortunately, **Cypress** and **Holly Creek Picnic Areas** offer opportunities to relax at the shaded tables by clear cool streams. If you are headed south, relax and enjoy!

The **Sunken Trace** exhibit at 1,000 feet in elevation marks the end of this long northbound ascent or the beginning of a mostly downhill journey south to the Tennessee River at 420 feet. A short walk off the Parkway clearly reveals three rutted paths created by travelers who rerouted the Trace in order to avoid mudholes. A short distance north is the site of the **McGlamery Stand** where many Kaintucks received meals and a night's rest. By continuing on the road past the interpretive marker, you will soon see a fire tower that you may climb (at your own risk, of course) for a bird's eye view of the Highland Rim.

The small town of **Collinwood**, conveniently located next to Parkway, is your best opportunity for purchasing groceries between Tupelo and Nashville. The local inhabitants are certainly accustomed to seeing hungry cyclists rolling through the small Main Street in search of groceries and a Southern cookin' restaurant.

North of Collinwood, both **Sweetwater** and **Glenrock Branches** offer more shady rest stops by clear gurgling creeks. The adventurous cyclists might opt to take the **Old Trace Drive** which winds along a densely forested ridge with occasional overlooks. This narrow bumpy lane is mostly paved, but watch for gravel as you taste the old Trace of a bygone era.

Between the Old Trace Drive and Meriwether Lewis Historic Site, three back-to-back moderate climbs between 150 and 200 feet await cyclists pedaling in either direction.

Just admire the scenery and enjoy the fast downhills between the climbs.

A stop at the **Napier Mine** reveals a large pit mine where iron ore was extracted from the red soil. The Napier Ironworks operated in this area from the mid-19th century until the 1920s. Workers using picks and shovels loaded the iron ore in mule-drawn carts that hauled it to iron furnaces.

The **Metal Ford Historic Site** lies just south of the Buffalo River and is well worth the .8-mile roundtrip detour from the Parkway. The rock bluffs, mature hardwoods, and the cascading shoals of the Buffalo River make this a wonderful place to relax (and a popular local swimming and fishing hole). The rocky shoals served as a shallow ford during the Boatmen's Era. There were no bridges in the early days of the Trace, and travelers had to use shallow crossings such as this one to continue their journey north. In the 1820s, the river was harnessed to power the charcoal furnaces of the Steele's Iron Works. Nothing remains of this pig iron furnace today except for the chute that diverted water.

If you can arrange a layover day (or even half a day) near here, try canoeing the Buffalo River. Jim Hobbs of **Buffalo River Canoeing** (800/339-5596) can arrange to meet you here or pick you up nearby and send you on a relaxing float down this peaceful untamed river. Ann and I have seen turtles, fish, snakes, herons, kingfishers, deer, and beavers while we drifted among the rocky cliffs and forested banks. The swift current makes some of the bends rather tricky, but this Class I river is still suitable for beginners.

North of the Buffalo, one final climb leads you to the **Meriwether Lewis Historic Site** located .4 mile from the Parkway. In 1803, Captain Lewis and Captain William Clark left St. Louis with 26 soldiers for a daring 9,000-mile journey to the Pacific Coast and back. Upon returning to Washington, D.C. in 1807, Lewis was commissioned as governor of the Louisiana Territory. On his northward journey on the Trace to Washington, D.C., Lewis mysteriously died of a gunshot wound on October 11, 1809 at the age of 35. Was it murder or suicide? It is unlikely we will ever know what happened that night at Grinders Stand. Today a large monument marks his grave, and a reconstruction of the stand serves as a small museum. A 3-mile roundtrip leads to the campground and a secluded picnic area along Little Swan Creek. There are also several miles of hiking trails including sections on the Old Trace.

From the Lewis site, TN 20 connects with two unique destinations on either side of the Parkway. Six miles to the west lies the town of **Hohenwald**, originally a Swiss-German settlement that now boasts various shops, restaurants, a unique museum, and a motel. Twelve miles to the east, you'll find **The Farm**, a vegetarian co-op community which was founded in 1971 by philosopher Steve Gaskin. Cottage industries include an ecovillage, a soy dairy, and a midwife center. A camping area, dormitory-style lodging, and B&B accommodate all types of travelers. If you have extra time, a swimming hole and trails for hiking and mountain biking are also on the property. (See map on p. 166).

Milepost

328.0   Pickwick Lake. This lake was created in 1938 when the Tennessee Valley Authority dammed the Tennessee River.

328.7   Lauderdale Picnic Area

329.0   CR 2. Florence is 17 mi. east. (See mp 331.9 for lodging info.)

330.2   Rock Springs. Nature trail to cold water spring and beaver dams.

331.9   AL 14 (**Cpg**). Brush Creek County Park Campground (no showers) and an adjacent **Mkt/Rst** are 6 mi. west on AL 14. Hart Campground (256/768-1555) (showers, laundry) is 13 mi. west. Florence (**Supermkt, Rst, Ldg, Bike Shop**) is 15 mi. east. (See *Florence Loop* for route and www.visitflorenceal.com or 888/FLO-TOUR for lodging info.)

336.3	AL 20. Busy highway to Florence. Use CR 14 or CR 2.
341.8	Alabama-Tennessee Line. This boundary along the 35th parallel dates back to 1735.
342.3	**Mkt.** A market with a few non-perishable foods is .5 mi. east on this unmarked road. Go right at the T-stop.
343.2	Cypress Creek Picnic Area
346.2	Holly Picnic Area
350.5	Sunken Trace. Rutted remnants of the original Trace show how it was relocated to avoid mudholes.
351.0	TN 13 (**Mkt, Cpg**) Four Mile Market and Campground (no showers) is just off the parkway.
352.9	McGlamery Stand. Site of an inn along the Trace. You may climb the state forest firetower (at own risk) for a bird's eye view.
354.9	TN 13/Collinwood (**W, RR, Mkt, Visitors Center, Supermkt, Rst, Ldg, Cpg**). A visitors center (with showers) is located just west of the Parkway. A convenience market is .5 mi. west of the Parkway. A mid-size supermarket is just beyond after turning left on TN 13. Free camping for cyclists is permitted in the city park. Miss Monetta's Country Cottage $ (931/724-9309) and Rochell's Rooms $ (931/724-9119) are located in town. **Last reliable water southbound for 28 miles.**
363.0	Sweetwater Branch. A short nature trail meanders through the forest along this clear, fast-flowing stream. Beautiful wildflowers in season.
364.5	Lower Glenrock Branch Picnic Area (**W, RR**). Shaded tables are situated by a sparkling brook that has carved lovely rock bluffs. A trail leads to Upper Glenrock Branch.
367.3	Dogwood Mudhole. This portion of the original Trace was often impassable after heavy rains.
370.3	US 64 (**Mkt, Rst, Ldg**). Market just west of the Parkway has a fair selection of canned and packaged goods plus a deli and some hot meals. A motel, restaurants, and a supermarket are 10 mi. west in Waynesboro (see p. 153 for lodging info or www.waynecountychamber.org) on the wide-shouldered US 64.

372.6   Laurel Hill Lake and Wildlife Management Area
(**Rst**, **Cpg**). A campground (no showers) is 2
mi. east. Turn left on Peter Cave Rd. (dirt) at
1.7 mi. There is also a lunch counter at the dock
near the campground. Rowboat rentals.

375.8   Old Trace Drive. This roughly paved narrow lane
follows the original Trace for 2.5 mi. Watch for
gravel if you decide to take it.

377.8   Jack's Branch Picnic Area (**W**, **RR**). Another shady
haven by a crystal clear creek.

380.8   Napier Rd. (**Mkt**, **Cpg**, **Ldg**). The Natchez Trace
Wilderness Preserve (showers, laun-
dry)(931/796-3212), a membership campground resort, is 1 mi. east of the Parkway.
Non-members are welcome if space is available. Features fishing and boating lake, swimming pool, cabins, and market. Buffalo River
Canoeing (931/796-2211 or 800/339-5596) can
sometimes arrange to shuttle cyclists to their
campgrounds (showers) 13 miles off the Trace.

381.8   Napier Mine. View of an open pit mine where iron
ore was extracted using hand tools.

382.8   Metal Ford. A .8-mi. roundtrip takes you to a scenic
area by the Buffalo River. Also site of an ironworks and the Mclish's Stand.

385.9   Meriwether Lewis Historic Site/TN 20 (**W**, **Mkt**,
Ldg, **Cpg**). A reconstruction of the Grinder's
Inn houses a small museum. Pay phone and
water are adjacent. The Lewis monument and
gravesite are just beyond. A 3 mi. roundtrip
leads to the campground (no showers) and a
picnic area along Little Swan Creek. A market
with a fair selection of canned and packaged
goods is 1.7 mi. east of the Parkway on TN 20.
Restaurants, supermarket, and lodging available 6 miles away in Hohenwald. Embassy Inn
$ (931/796-1500). Camping (with showers),
dormitory-type lodging $, and a B&B $ are also
available at The Farm located 12 mi. to the east.
Take TN 20 east, then left on Drakes Ln. (not
well marked—see map on p. 166). Advance
arrangements required (931/964-3574).

MERIWETHER LEWIS TO
NORTHERN TERMINUS
mp 386-442

Highlights: Phosphate Mine, Fall Hollow, Swan View
Overlook, Sheboss Place, Tobacco Barn, Jackson
Falls, Baker Bluff, Gordon House and Ferry Site
(Duck River), Water Valley Overlook, Tennessee
Valley Divide, TN 96 bridge.
Terrain: Several tough climbs, but plenty of gently
rolling ridgetop terrain.
Northbound Elevation: 470 ft. difference; 2,130 ft.
accumulated; 38 ft. average per mile.
Southbound Elevation: 470 ft. difference; 2,040 ft.
accumulated; 36 ft. average per mile.
Camping: TN 412 (mp 391), TN 50 (mp 408).
Lodging: TN 412 (mp 391), Trace Haven (mp 401),
Hwy 7 (mp 416), Leipers Fork (mp 429).

With two waterfalls, three overlooks, and miles of
deciduous forests, the northernmost section of the Trace
offers gorgeous scenery in addition to historic sites, but you
will have to work for it! If you haven't used your low gear
by now, you will definitely need it here. Northbound from
Meriwether Lewis Historic Site, a fun descent is followed
by a particularly challenging upgrade (300 feet in one mile)
to the **Swan Valley Overlook.** The southbound traveler will
no doubt relish this downhill which is probably the fastest
descent on the Trace. More than once, I temporarily aborted
this climb to stand under the cool falls at **Fall Hollow** on a
sweltering summer afternoon.

Another picturesque waterfall along the Parkway
formed when the Duck River eroded a rocky bluff above
a bend in the river. The upper portion of Irvin Creek
changed its course and tumbled over this rocky ledge,

creating **Jackson Falls.** A short paved trail leads to the double-terraced falls located in a rugged forested hollow. Both these intermittent waterfalls are only a trickle during dry periods.

Baker Bluff, just to the north of Jackson Falls, overlooks an environmentally-conscious farm, and a sign explains how the layout of the farm helps it live in harmony with the land. From this bluff, the Parkway quickly drops onto a flood plain and crosses the Duck River. On a misty autumn night under a full moon, my wife and I had the good fortune to witness a ghostly white moonbow spanning across the river.

A sheltered rest area is located at the site of the **Gordon Ferry**. John Gordon was a renowned Indian fighter who fought battles ranging from Ft. Nashboro (Nashville) to the Seminole Wars in Florida. He was also the first postmaster of Nashville. His wife, Dorothea, operated the ferry across the Duck River under agreement with Chickasaw Chief George Colbert while her husband was away at war. The two-story brick Gordon home, built in 1818, sits adjacent to

Water Valley Overlook

the picnic shelter.

A gradual 250-foot grade lasting 2.5 miles leads north to the Duck River Ridge. From here, the **Water Valley Overlook** offers one of the best views from the Natchez Trace. The *Snow Creek Loop* runs through this peaceful rural valley that spreads out below. The Parkway crosses the **Tennessee Valley Divide** (mp 424), a long ridge approximately 1,000 feet high separating the watersheds of the Tennessee and Cumberland Rivers. The Kaintucks and other travelers were greatly relieved when they crossed north over this ridge that marked the boundary between Indian Territory and the United States. If you are pedaling south, you will also be relieved that you have conquered the last big hill until after you cross the Duck River 16 miles later. For nine miles north of the divide, the Trace is moderately hilly in either direction.

Leipers Fork, a small community along TN 46, is a town rich in history. Originally known as Hillsboro, it was settled in the 1780s by the Leiper brothers, one of whom died in the Battle of the Bluffs at Ft. Nashboro (1781). In 1800, Thomas Hart Benton, the famous senator from Missouri was brought here as a child by his widowed mother. He eventually left Nashville with his brother Jesse who had shot and wounded future-President Andrew Jackson in a brawl.

The original Trace followed what is now TN 46 East (Old Hillsboro Rd.). Today, many country music stars live in the area, and stately mansions and white limousines are not an uncommon site.

You will hardly notice that you are approaching Nashville during the last 20 miles of the Parkway. Heading north from TN 46, the Natchez Trace gradually rises 230 feet onto Backbone Ridge which separates the Harpeth and South Harpeth Rivers. The Parkway becomes very windy (speed limit is now 40 mph) as it meanders along the thickly forested hilltops, offering occasional views of the surrounding countryside.

If the new Natchez Trace has made history, it might be for the magnificent **double arch bridge over TN 96**. The $14 million dollar bridge, the only arch bridge built without using spandrel columns, spans a length of five football fields (1, 572 feet) at a height of 155 feet above the valley floor. Be sure to stop at the overlook at the north side of the bridge to view this engineering marvel.

TN 96 Bridge

The Trace continues along Backbone Ridge before descending to its final terminus at TN 100. If you're starting a southbound trek, the Parkway welcomes you with a steep 270-foot climb within two miles. The site of the future visitor center is at the top of the hill just two miles south of the terminus. Next to the terminus sits the Loveless Cafe, a favorite among locals for many years. This country-style eatery, famous for its biscuits and country ham, has served many country music stars in addition to hungry cyclists.

From the terminus, TN 100 heads toward Nashville providing cyclists with narrow, but generally usable, paved shoulders. This highway is fairly busy, especially during commute hours. I suggest using *Option 2* or *Option 3* in the next chapter (unless you absolutely must ride the entire Trace). Besides being more peaceful, these scenic routes pass interesting historic landmarks and often follow the original path of the Trace.

Milepost

390.7   Phosphate Mine. A 5-minute walk follows an old railbed to the collapsed entrance of the mine which was part of a system of mines centered around nearby Gordonsburg. During the late 19th century, African-Americans and Italian immigrants worked the mines that provided a valuable source of fertilizer for Southern farmers.

391.1   US 412 (**Cpg, Ldg**). The Fall Hollow Campground (showers)(931/796-1480) is located at the parkway exit. Also has has two rooms with double beds and can provide meals with advance notice. The Embassy Inn $ (931/796-1500) is located 6 miles west in Hohenwald (also restaurants and supermarket). Ridgetop B&B $$ (931/285-2777) is located 4 mi. east on TN 412. Shuttles can be arranged. Southbound cyclists may take wide-shouldered US 412 west to lodging, restaurants, and supermarket in Hohenwald.

391.9   Fall Hollow. A paved path leads to an overlook of a small creek plunging 20 feet into a clear pool. A dirt trail continues to the base of the falls.

392.5   Swan View Overlook

394.1   Devil's Backbone State Natural Area. Hiking trails meander among the rugged hills and hollows.

400.2   Sheboss Place. A stand owned by an Indian married to an Anglo wife was located here. Not knowing any English, he would tell travelers to talk to her instead of him by saying "She boss."

401.4   Tobacco Farm and Old Trace Drive (**Ldg**). An old barn is used to explain the growing of tobacco. Be sure to take in the wonderful view from behind the barn. A 2-mile ride (one-way northbound) on the Old Trace takes you along a narrow shady lane before rejoining the Parkway. Near this point, cyclists can walk off the Parkway to Trace Haven $$ (931/583-2714), a lovely cabin on 80 acres owned by bicycle enthusiasts Sherry Littley and Tony Belcher.

404.7   Jackson Falls (**W, RR, PS**). A short paved trail leads down a steep narrow hollow to a cascading waterfall named after Andrew Jackson.

405.1   Baker Bluff. A sign explains the earth-friendly agricultural techniques that are employed on the farm. The overlook, situated directly above the Duck River, provides an excellent view of the rural landscape.

407.2   Duck River

407.7   Gordon House and Ferry Site (**W, RR, PS**). From this two-story brick home built in 1818, Dorothea, the wife of renowned Indian fighter John Gordon, operated a ferry across the Duck River under agreement with Chickasaw Chief George Colbert.

408.0   TN 50/Junction of Adventure Cycling's *Great River Route* and TN DOT's *Heartland Route* (see *Appendices*). (**Mkt, Cpg**). Market, fairly well-stocked with canned and dry goods plus deli, is 1 mi. west. A cyclist-only camping area (no showers) is located at the trailhead just west of the Parkway. Use restrooms at Gordon House and Ferry Site.

411.8   Water Valley Overlook

415.7   TN 7 (**Mkt, Ldg**). There is a long downhill for most of the 2 mi. to this market east of the NTP. (Guess what that means...) The market is reasonably stocked with canned and packaged goods. Creekview Farm Retreat $$-$$$ (931/682-2775) is located 3 mi. away.

423.8   Tennessee Valley Divide. This ridge, 1,000 ft. in elevation, marked the boundary of the Indian territory to the south and U.S. territory to the north.

425.0   Burns Branch. Picnic tables along a clear cold creek.

427.5   Garrison Creek (**W, RR, PS**). This creek was named after the army garrison that camped near here while "improving" the Trace. Hiking trails lead to an overlook of the valley and continue along the ridge.

429.0   TN 46/*Bike route to Franklin and Nashville* (**Mkt, Rst, Ldg**). Town of Leipers Fork. A market, reasonably stocked with canned and packaged goods, is 1 mi. east on TN 46. Turn left at the T-stop (still TN 46) and continue another mile to reach the center of Leipers Fork with a restaurant, small grocery/deli with some meat and produce. Namaste B&B $$$ (615/791-0333) is located 1.8 mi. south of the stop sign. Additional lodging/restaurants located 9 mi. away in Franklin (see p. 123).

437.4   TN 96/*Bike route to Franklin and Nashville*

438.0   TN 96 Bridge and Overlook

439.4   Backbone Ridge Overlook

439.9   Future Visitor Center

442.2   Northern Terminus/TN 100/*Bike route to Nashville* (**Mkt, Rst, Bike Shop**).

NATCHEZ TRACE PARKWAY TO NASHVILLE

Highlights: Fort Nashborough, 2nd Avenue, Ryman Auditorium, Gen. Jackson Riverboat, State Capitol, Bicentennial Mall, Country Music Hall of Fame and Music Row, Opryland Hotel, Andrew Jackson's Hermitage, Centennial Park, Belle Meade Mansion, Warner Parks.
Terrain: Rarely flat but mostly gentle grades.
Camping: None available between Nashville and mp 408 on the Parkway (see p. 112).
Lodging: Numerous motels and hotels within 5 miles of downtown Nashville. Motels and B&B's also available in Franklin.

Nashville, or "Music City, USA" as many affectionately call it, makes a great place to begin or end your bike tour. Whether you like bluegrass, country music, jazz, blues, or rock, you'll find it here. Music City also lives up to its name with excellent opera, ballet, and symphonic music.

If you've just finished cycling the 450-mile Natchez Trace Parkway, food may interest you more than culture, and we don't blame you one bit! From barbecue to vegetarian, Nashville has a greater variety of dining than any other city along the Trace. While the honky-tonks on Lower Broad still draw the crowds, coffee houses and micro-breweries are surprisingly abundant in the country music capital.

A replica of **Fort Nashborough** (open to the public; no admission) is situated on the bluff above the Cumberland River at Nashville's riverfront. During the unusually frigid winter of 1779-80, a group of settlers led by James Robertson arrived at the river's edge and crossed on the ice. They hastily built a settlement surrounded by a stockade. Five months later, John Donelson arrived with the rest of the settlers by flatboat, having navigated the Tennessee, Ohio, and Cumberland Rivers. This wilderness outpost, along with others that were established nearby during the 1780s, was vulnerable to Indian attack. In the spring of 1781, the men fell into a well-planned ambush, but the quick-thinking Mrs. Robertson averted a massacre by releasing the snarling and growling dogs. The frightened Indians retreated, allowing the settlers to return to the fort. As the Indian hostilities subsided in the 1790s, agriculture prospered, and the stockade was replaced with a growing village.

Today the village is still growing, and **Second Avenue** is the hot spot in town. These renovated brick buildings were originally markets and warehouses during the steamboat days. The Hard Rock Cafe and the Wild Horse Saloon (where you can learn line dancing) are the major attractions along with numerous restaurants, bars, and clubs that cater to locals and tourists alike. You'll find additional dining and nightlife nearby on Broadway, known as "**Lower Broad**."

The majestic **Tennessee State Capitol** (1855) proudly occupies the high ground on the hill even as the modern skyscrapers rise above it. To the north, the capitol building

Riverfront Park in downtown Nashville

overlooks the **Farmers' Market** and **Bicentennial Mall** (a landscaped promenade dedicated to the state's 200th birthday in 1996). Another magnificent building is the **Union Station** (currently a hotel and restaurant) built of stone in 1900 by the Louisville & Nashville Railroad.

The **Ryman Auditorium**, built in 1892, is located on 4th Avenue and Broadway. Originally built for religious revivals by steamboat Captain Tom Ryman, it was later used by WSM to host the "WSM Barndance." The radio show became the "Grand Ole Opry," the longest running radio broadcast in the country. This historic building was renovated in the 1990s and currently hosts a variety of shows.

Should you desire to attend the present day "Grand Ole Opry" on Friday and Saturday nights, you'll have to go to **Opryland**. In addition to the 4,000 seat theater, you'll also find Opry Mills, a huge shopping complex and one of the largest hotel and convention centers in the country. One part of the hotel surrounds the Cascades, a multi-story greenhouse with waterfalls, palm trees, and other tropical plants. The hotel's Delta section features a boat ride among trees and plants of the Mississippi Delta. Call 615/889-6611 for general information on Opryland.

For a pleasant bicycle excursion, head to the Schermerhorn Symphony Center (on 4th Ave. just south of Broadway) and cross the Shelby Street Pedestrian Bridge and follow the bike route/bike lanes along 1st St. and Davidson Dr. to Shelby Park and Shelby Bottoms Greenway. After a 2.5-mile ride, you will reach a four-mile paved multi-use path along the Cumberland River which connects to a beautiful new bike/ped bridge across the Cumberlad River which in turn leads to several more miles of cycling on the the Stones River Greenway.

Andrew Jackson's **Hermitage**, home of the seventh President of the United States, is located fifteen miles east of downtown. Jackson traveled the Natchez Trace several times before becoming president. His trips include marrying his beloved Rachel Donelson Robards near Natchez, negotiating treaties with the Choctaw and Chickasaw, and triumphantly defeating the British in 1815 at the Battle of New Orleans. Although he was a hero to many, his presidency was full of controversies ranging from nullifying Indian treaties to violating abolitionists' first amendment rights.

Jackson's lovely plantation home was built during his presidency (1829-37) and replaced a more modest home destroyed by fire. In addition to the house, Rachel's garden, the original log home, and outbuildings give us a glimpse of life on a Tennessee plantation. (Admission charged.)

Between downtown and the Natchez Trace Parkway, several attractions give ample opportunity to stop pedaling and see the sights. From West End Avenue, you can momentarily escape the traffic by turning into **Centennial Park** and enjoying a brief spin on the one-way roads around the **Parthenon**. Yes, that's right. Nashville boasts the only exact-size replica of the Greek Parthenon. Inside you'll find an art museum and an impressive two-story statue of the Athena.

Known as the queen of the Tennessee plantations, the 1853 Greek-revival **Belle Meade Plantation** makes another worthwhile stop *en route* to the Parkway. The large carriage house and stables were home to the famous racehorse Iroquois, first American horse to win the English Derby. A 1790s log cabin that was the original family home is also on the grounds. From this cabin on the original Natchez Trace, the Harding family saw numerous boatmen who were, no doubt, relieved to have finished the perilous wilderness trek. (Admission charged for touring the mansion; no admission for touring the grounds.)

If you want to add 2-3 extra miles (and some respectable hills!) to the day's journey, take a spin through the **Warner Parks**, a 2,700 acre forested nature preserve and, in my opinion, one of the best short bike rides anywhere. The one-way main loop through Percy Warner Park features 11 miles of good pavement, extremely light traffic, and lots of curves and hills. The smaller Edwin Warner Park south of Old Hickory Boulevard has its own paved road system that is closed to motor traffic. With a little navigational effort, cyclists may utilize the park road system (see map on p. 207) along with Belle Meade Boulevard to avoid the traffic on Harding Road and TN 100. In addition to the hills, this detour will add 2.5 miles southbound or 3.5 miles northbound to your day's journey.

This guide includes three options connecting Nashville and the Natchez Trace Parkway. In all options, cyclists must contend with 12 miles of busy roads including Broadway, West End Avenue (which becomes Harding Road), TN 100, and Old Hickory Boulevard before reaching the pleasant rural roads connecting with the Parkway. Generally, these routes are not too bad for street-wise cyclists. Make every effort to be alert, be visible, obey traffic laws, and avoid rush hours. Fortunately, with three bike shops and a major college campus along West End Avenue, motorists are accustomed to seeing cyclists on these roads. Most of the busy portion of the route consists of a 4-lane highway which often, but not always, has paved shoulders or wide outside lanes.

While *Option 1* is the most direct route, a narrow four-mile stretch on TN 100 makes it less than ideal for cycling. This highway is everything you don't want—only one narrow lane in each direction, fast motorists, and heavy traffic. A narrow, but rideable shoulder has recently been added to make this route a little more tolerable. Although several local cyclists do ride this, I suggest using *Option 2* or *Option 3* which are much more enjoyable.

Option 2 follows the Harpeth River on a quaint section of the original Natchez Trace, passing Indian mounds, remains of an original stone bridge built in 1801, and two beautiful ante-bellum homes. It joins the Parkway at the colossal Highway 96 bridge. On two occasions Ann and I escorted Adventure Cycling Association tours on *Option 3* which also uses the original Trace along with peaceful coun try roads leading to Franklin. After visiting the town that claims to be the best preserved small town in Tennessee, you may reach the Parkway via TN 96 or follow the *Option 3* directions to Leipers Fork.

Pat Cox, owner of Lightning Cycles, takes a spin through Franklin

Downtown Dining

The following is not a complete list but a sampling of the variety of dining that is available.

The Arcade—runs between 4th and 5th Ave just south of Church St. (Mon.-Fri. 8 a.m. - 2:00) Several restaurants, shops, and a coffee house line this historic arcade.

12th and Porter—114 12th Ave. N. (Mon.-Thurs. 11-2, 5:30-10; Fri.- Sat. 5:30 -1 a.m.) Hidden off Broadway, this restaurant features pizza, pastas, seafood, and ethnic vegetarian cuisine. Adjacent night club has live music.

Big River Brewing Works and Grille—111 Broadway (Daily 11-11) Serves a variety of their own ales and stouts along with sandwiches, burgers, pasta, and salads.

Hard Rock Cafe—100 Broadway (Daily 11 a.m.- 2 a.m.) Hamburgers and other American favorites served with loud rock music.

Ichiban—109 2nd Ave. N. (Mon.-Fri. 11-2, 5-10; Sat.-Sun. 5-10) Japanese cuisine and sushi bar.

Jack's Barbecue—334 Broadway (Mon.-Wed. 10:30-3; Thurs.-Sat. 10:30-10) This little eatery in the shadow of the Ryman Auditorium has been serving barbecue for many years. Also features country bands in the evenings.

Market Street Brewery—124 Second Ave. N. (Daily 11-10) The first modern micro-brewery in Nashville makes a variety of ales, pilsners, bock, and seasonal beers. Serves sandwiches, burgers, and typical pub fare.

The Melting Pot—166 2nd Ave. N. (Daily 5 p.m.-midnight) This place will delight fondue lovers.

Seanachie Irish Pub & Restaurant—327 Broadway (Daily 11- midnight) Irish fare from corned beef to seafood.

Spaghetti Factory—160 2nd Ave. N. (Mon.-Fri. 11:30-2, 5-10; Sat. 4:30-11; Sun. 4-9:30) Serving lots of pasta for the buck, this eatery sits in a historic building on the old waterfront.

Union Station Hotel—1001 Broadway (Daily 6:30 a.m.-10 p.m.) In addition to the hotel, this grand old train station built in 1900 now houses the casual Broadway Bistro and the elegant Arthur's.

Wild Horse Saloon—120 2nd Ave. N. (Daily 11-10) Watch line dancing to "Achey-Breaky Heart" and other country favorites while enjoying a variety of American food.

Dining Between Downtown and I-440

2525 West End—Several options on the ground floor of the Vanderbilt Marriot Hotel that include Starbucks, Bread & Co., Borders Bookstore Deli and Espresso Bar, and P.F. Chang's Bistro. You will find something to eat from early morning through late evening.

Blackstone's—1918 West End Ave. (Mon.-Sat. 11-midnight; Sun. noon-10) This micro-brewery makes a variety of ales including a very popular dark porter. The menu includes pizza, seafood, steaks, and burgers.

Calypso Cafe—2424 Elliston Pl. (Mon.-Sat. 11-9; Sun. 12-8) Good Caribbean food (including vegetarian black beans) at good prices.

DaVinci's—1812 Hayes St.—near 18th Ave. one block west of West End Ave. (Daily 4:30 p.m.-10) The gourmet pizza is, in our opinion, some of the best anywhere.

Elliston Place Soda Shop—2111 Elliston Pl. (Mon.-Sat. 11-8) Right out of the 1950s, this diner with juke boxes on every table serves home-style meals. The sundaes and ice cream sodas are scrumptious.

SalaThai—2106 West End Ave. (Daily 10-10)

Tin Angel—3201 West End Ave. (Mon.-Thurs. 11-11; Fri. 11-midnight; Sat. 5-midnight) The variety of pasta, chicken, and salads served here will please the health-conscious cyclist.

Zola—3001 West End Ave (Mon.-Sat. 5:30 p.m.-10) Gourmet southern cuisine with Mediterranean influence. Includes vegetarian dishes.

Dining Between I-440 and the Parkway

Bread & Co.—6051 Hwy. 100 (Mon.-Fri. 8:30-7; Sat. 10-7; Sun. 12-5) Popular spot for local cyclists after pedaling the Warner Parks. Excellent soups, salads, and sandwiches, but the espresso brownies are our favorite.

Calypso Cafe—5101 Harding Pk. (Mon.-Sat. 11-9; Sun. 12-8) Good Caribbean food (including vegetarian black beans) at good prices.

Martha's at the Belle Meade Plantation—5025 Harding Rd. (Lunch daily; Dinner Thur.-Sat.) Popular lunch spot serving soup, sandwiches, and salads on the beautiful plantation grounds. Reservations (615/353-2828) recommended on weekends .

Finnezza Trattoria—(5404 Harding Rd. Mon.-Thurs. 5-10; Fri.-Sat. 5-11; Sun. 5-9) Creative Italian meals. Perfect for carbo-loading.

Loveless Cafe—8400 Hwy. 100 (Mon.-Sat. 8-2. 5-9; Sun. 8-9) This little cafe at the Parkway terminus has been a long-time favorite among locals and country music stars. While famous for its country ham, we go there for the biscuits and preserves. Reservations (call 615/646-9700) are usually needed on weekends.

Sportsman's Grille—5405 Harding Rd. (Daily 11-10) Features American food including some of the best fried catfish around.

Downtown Lodging

Crowne Plaza $$$ (615/259-2000 or 800/2CROWNE). Located near the state capitol. Short walk to all downtown attractions.

Days Inn Downtown $$ (615/242-4311 or 800/627-3297) Adjacent to the state capitol, this reasonably-priced hotel is within walking distance of downtown attractions.

Hermitage Hotel $$$ (615/244-3121or 800/251-1908) Opened in 1910 at a cost of $1 million, this historic hotel has hosted 6 presidents and numerous celebrities. Next to state capitol. Short walk to downtown attractions.

Renaissance Hotel $$$ (615/255-8400 or 800/468-3571) Located close to Broadway and 2nd Ave.

Shoneys Inn $$ (615/255-9977) Located on Music Row at the edge of downtown, guests can walk or take a trolley to Broadway and 2nd Ave.

Union Station Hotel $$$ (615/726-1001or 800/331-2123) This beautiful stone building with clock tower was the elegant train depot in the railroad era.

Lodging Between Downtown and I-440

Days Inn West End $$ (615/327-0922 or 800/DAYSINN). Located near Vanderbilt University. Bike shops and restaurants nearby.

Daisy Hill B&B $$-$$$ (615/383-0426) Located in a historic neighborhood near Vanderbilt University. Close to restaurants and bike shops.

Hampton Inn Vanderbilt $$-$$$ (615/329-1144 or 800/HAMPTON) Located near Vanderbilt University. Bike shops and restaurants nearby.

Holiday Inn at Vanderbilt $$$ (615/327-4707 or 800/HOLIDAY) Located near Vanderbilt University. Bike shops and restaurants nearby.

Guesthouse Inn & Suites $$ (615/329-1000 or 800/777-4904) Located near Vanderbilt University. Bike shops and restaurants nearby.

Lodging between I-440 and the Natchez Trace

Apple Brook B&B $$ (615/646-5082) 1896 farmhouse located 2.5 mi. west of the terminus on TN 100. Can somet imes arrange airport shuttles.

Baymont Inn & Suites $$ (615/353-0700 or 800/301-0200) 2 mi. off the route on White Bridge Rd.

Comfort Inn $$ (615/356-0888 or 800/228-5150) 2 mi.off route on White Bridge Rd.

Days Inn $-$$ (615/356-9100 or 800/329-7466) 1.5 mi. off route on White Bridge Rd.

Franklin Restaurants

Antonio's—119 5th Ave. N. (Mon.-Sat., dinner). Fine Italian cuisine.
Dotson's—99 E. Main St. (Mon.-Sat. 6 a.m.-8:30 p.m.; Sun. 7-2:30 p.m.)
A popular meat n' three with delicious homemade pies.
Dumplin's of Franklin—4th and Main (lunch daily) Known for its
"comfort foods" such as casseroles, chicken salads, pasta, and more.
The Factory—230 Franklin Rd. An eclectic mix of shops and restaurants
in an historic stove factory.
Hunan—413 Main St. (Daily 11:30-9) Chinese cuisine.
La Hacienda—Del Rio Pk. and US 431 (Daily 11-10) Mexican cuisine.
Merridee's—110 4th Ave S. (Mon.-Sat. 7:30-5) This bakery is a popular
destination for Nashville cyclists. They also serve soups, sandwiches, and
gourmet coffee.
Plantation—109 S. Margin St. (Daily 10-10). Chicken, pizza, etc. cooked
in a fire oven.
Sandy's Grill—108 4th Ave S. (Mon.-Sat. lunch and dinner) Seafood and
Southern gourmet.
Starbucks—Main and 5th (Open daily) Breakfast, lunch, and coffee.

Franklin Lodging

Baymont Inn & Suites $-$$ (615/791-7700 or 800/301-0200) Located on
TN 96 near I-65.
Best Western $-$$ (615/790-0570 or 800/251-3200) Located on TN 96 near I-65.
Comfort Inn $-$$ (615/791-6675 or 800/228-5150) Located on TN 96
near I-65.
Days Inn $-$$ (615/790-1140 or 800/DAYSINN) Located on TN 96 near I-65.
Holiday Inn Express $$ (615/591-6660 or 800/HOLIDAY) Located on
TN 96 near I-65.
Magnolia House B&B $$$ (615/794-8178) Historic home near Carter House
just south of town square.
Old Marshall House B&B $$-$$$ (615/591-4121 or 800/863-5808) 1869
Victorian farmhouse located in a rural setting near TN 96 and I-65.
Rebel's Roost B&B $$$ (615/790-8346) 1866 home near town square.

Note: Cyclists wishing to avoid some of busy West End Ave.
may use the signed bikeway system through Music Row
(where the recording studios are). From downtown Nash-
ville, use Demonbreun St., Music Sq./16th Ave (or Music
Sq./17th Ave inbound), Magnolia Blvd., Fairfax Ave (or
Blair/Chesterfield Ave. and 21st Ave. inbound), Marlboro
Ave., and Elmington Ave. to reach West End just past I-440.
Visit www.walkbikenashivlle.org for online maps and other
information on the bikeway system.

Natchez Trace Parkway to Nashville (Northbound)

Begin at Option 1, Option 2, or Option 3

Option 1

Mile

0.0 **Right** on the TN 100 exit at mp 442.2.

0.2 **Right** on TN 100 (toward Nashville) at the end of the access road (**Mkt, Rst, Bike Shop**). Trace Bikes (615/646-2485) is on the left. Caution—narrow 2-lane highway with fast traffic for next 4 miles.

2.5 **Supermkt, Rst**

4.1 Straight at Old Hickory Blvd. (traffic light).

4.8 Straight at Old Hickory Blvd. (traffic light) (**W, RR**). Water and restrooms at the nature center just before this intersection.

Go to All Options

Option 2

0.0 **Right** on the TN 96 exit at mp 437.4. Cyclists may reach Franklin on TN 96 and join *Option 3*. Distance to Franklin is 9 mi.

0.6 **Right** on TN 96 going east.

4.1 **Left** on TN 46/Old Hillsboro Rd. (flashing yellow light).

6.4 **Left** on Old Natchez Trace (easy to miss).

10.5 **Right** on Sneed Rd. (stop sign).

11.0 **Left** on Vaughn Rd. (easy to miss).

12.8 Edwin Warner Park (**W, RR**—except in winter, **PS**).

13.2 **Left** on Old Hickory Blvd. (traffic light) To detour through Percy Warner Park, take the road straight ahead for .4 mi. to the Main Drive. (See *Percy Warner Park Loop*.)

14.0 **Right** on TN 100 (traffic light)(**W, RR**). Turn left for water and restrooms at nature center.

Go to All Options

Option 3

0.0   Exit onto TN 46/Pinewood Rd. at mp 429.

0.3   **Right** on TN 46 going east at the end of the access road.

0.9   **Left** on Old Hillsboro Rd./TN 46 Rd. (stop sign at T-intersection)(**Mkt, Rst, Ldg**—see p. 113).

2.4   **Right** on Southall Rd./Old Hwy. 96.

6.2   **Left** on TN 246/Carters Creek Pk. (stop sign at T-intersection)(**Mkt**). This road becomes Main St. as you enter Franklin.

9.1   **Rst, Mkt, Laundry.**

10.1   **Right**, staying on TN 246, where Main St. becomes one-way in the opposing direction (or walk your bike for one block to 5th Ave/US 431).

10.2   **Left** on US 431/5th Ave. (traffic light).

10.3   Cross Main St. and continue on US 431/5th Ave. at the traffic light (**Rst, Ldg, Bike Shop**). Historic Franklin is to the right on Main St. Franklin Bicycle Co. (615/790-2702) is 2.5 mi. east on TN 96.

10.8   **Left** on Del Rio Pk. (traffic light)(**Supermkt, Rst**).

12.6   **Right**, staying on Del Rio Pk., at the stop sign.

14.2   **Left**, staying on Del Rio Pk., at the stop sign.

16.1   **Right** on TN 46/Old Hillsboro Rd. (stop sign at the T-intersection).

16.2   **Left** on Old Natchez Trace (first left).

20.3   **Right** on Sneed Rd. (stop sign).

20.8   **Left** on Vaughn Rd. (easy to miss).

22.6   Edwin Warner Park (**W/RR**—closed in winter, **PS**).

23.0   **Left** on Old Hickory Blvd. (traffic light). To detour through Percy Warner Park, take the road straight ahead for .4 mi. to the Main Drive. (See *Percy Warner Park Loop.*)

23.8   **Right** on TN 100 (traffic light)(**W, RR**). Turn left for water and restrooms at nature center.

Go to All Options

All Options

8.1, 17.3, 27.1	Continue straight where TN 100 joins US 70S/Harding Rd. (**Supermkt, Rst, Camping Store, Bike Shop**).Gran Fondo Bicycles (615/354-1090) is on your right.
8.5, 17.7, 27.5	Belle Meade Plantation (**Rst**).
10.3, 19.5, 29.3	Cross Woodmont/White Bridge Rd. (traffic light) (**Supermkt, Rst, Ldg**). Harding Rd. becomes West End Ave. Additional restaurants can be reached by going left on White Bridge Rd. The Baymont Inn, Comfort Inn, and Days Inn are 2 mi. to the left.
12.2, 21.4, 31.2	Cross over I-440.
12.8, 22.0, 31.8	**Supermkt, Rst, Bike Shop, Laundry.** Cumberland Transit (bikes/camping)(615/327-2453), Bike Pedlar (615/329-2453) are located within a block of 28th Ave.
13.1, 22.3, 32.1	Centennial Park (**Rst, Ldg**). Elliston Place (several unique restaurants/clubs) is one block north of via 24th or 23rd Ave.
14.0, 23.2, 33.0	West End Ave. merges with Broadway.
14.3, 23.5, 33.3	Cross over I-40 (Use caution).
14.8, 24.0, 33.8	8th Ave/Downtown Nashville (**Rst, Ldg**). See lodging/dining listings.

Nashville to Natchez Trace Parkway (Southbound)

Mile

0.0	From 8th and Broadway in downtown Nashville, bike west on Broadway/US 70S/US 431 (**Rst, Ldg**). The bus station is to the left on 8th Ave.
0.5	Cross I-40. (Caution: Busy right turn lane.)
0.8	Bear **right** onto West End Ave. where Broadway angles to the left (**Rst, Ldg**).

1.7 Centennial Park (**Rst, Ldg**). Elliston Place (several unique restaurants/clubs) is one block north (to the right) via 24th or 23rd Ave.

2.0 **Supermkt, Rst, Bike Shop, Laundry.** Cumberland Transit (bikes/camping)(615/327-2453), Bike Pedlar (615/329-2453) are within 1 block.

2.5 Cross over I-440. (Caution—busy right turn lane onto Murphy Rd./I-440. You may dismount and use the sidewalk/crosswalk.)

4.5 Cross Woodmont/White Bridge Rd. (**Supermkt, Rst, Ldg**). Additional restaurants can be reached by going right on White Bridge Rd. Motels are 2 mi. to the right.

5.0 Belle Meade Blvd. Go left for scenic detour through Warner Parks. See *Percy Warner Park Loop.*

6.3 Belle Meade Plantation (**Rst, Bike Shop**). Several restaurants in the next mile. Gran Fondo Bicycles (615/354-1090) will be on your left.

6.7 Bear left onto TN 100. (**Rst, Supermkt**) (Caution— you'll need to get in the left lane. Cross traffic does not stop.)

8.5 Entrance to Percy Warner Park (**PS**—no water).
Go to Option 1, Option 2, or Option 3

Option 1

10.0 Straight at Old Hickory Blvd. (traffic light) (**W, RR**—at nature center).

10.7 Straight at Old Hickory Blvd. (traffic light). Caution— busy narrow highway for next 4 miles.

12.3 **Supermkt, Rst**

14.6 **Mkt, Rst, Bike Shop**. Trace Bikes (615/646-2485) will be on your right.

14.8 **Right** on NTP after the Parkway bridge.

Option 2

10.0 **Left** on Old Hickory Blvd. (traffic light) (**W, RR**—.2 mi. ahead on TN 100 at nature center).

10.8 **Right** on Vaughn Rd. (traffic light) (**W/RR**— closed in winter, **PS**).

13.0 **Right** on Sneed Rd. (stop sign at T-intersection).

13.5 **Left** on Old Natchez Trace after crossing Harpeth River.
17.6 **Right** on Old Hillsboro Rd./TN 46 (stop sign at T-intersection).
19.9 **Right** on TN 96 (flashing red light).
23.4 **Left** on the NTP access road (steep .6 mi. climb).

Option 3

10.0 **Left** on Old Hickory Blvd. (traffic light) (**W, RR**— .2 mi. ahead on TN 100 at nature center).
10.8 **Right** on Vaughn Rd. (traffic light) (**W/RR**—closed in winter, **PS**).
13.0 **Right** on Sneed Rd. (stop sign at T-intersection).
13.5 **Left** on Old Natchez Trace after crossing Harpeth River.
17.6 **Right** on Old Hillsboro Rd./TN 46 (stop sign at T-intersection).
17.7 **Left** on Del Rio Pk. (first left).
19.6 **Right** (staying on Del Rio Pk.) at the 3-way stop.
21.2 **Left** (staying on Del Rio Pk.) at the next 3-way stop.
23.0 **Right** on US 431/5th Ave. (stop sign at T-intersection). (**Supermkt, Rst**). Cyclists may take TN 96 west for 9 mi. to the NTP.
23.5 **Right** on West Main St. (traffic light) (**Rst, Ldg, Bike Shop**). Take the street furthest to the right at this 5-way intersection. Historic Franklin is to the left at this intersection. Franklin Bicycle Co. (615/790-2702) is 2.5 mi. east on TN 96. Main St. becomes Carter Creek Pk. as you leave Franklin.
24.0 **Mkt, Rst, Laundry**.
27.5 **Right** on Southall Rd. (stop sign) (**Mkt**).
31.3 **Left** on TN 46/Old Hillsboro Rd. (stop sign at T-intersection)(**Mkt, Rst, Ldg**). See p. 113 for services.
32.8 **Right** on TN 46/Pinewood Rd.
33.5 **Left** on the NTP access road.

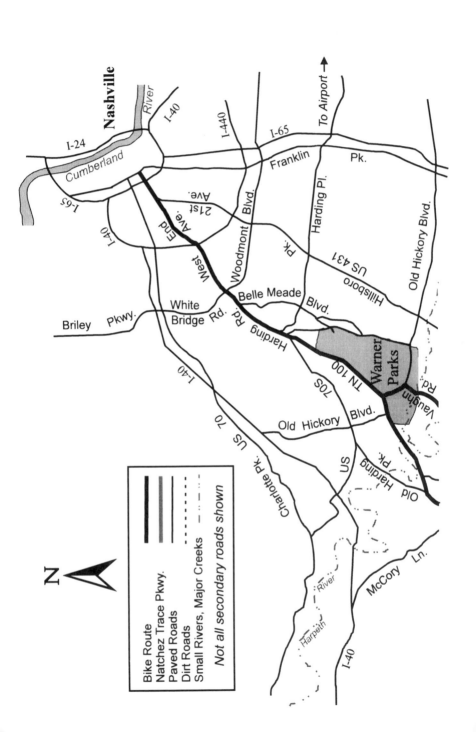

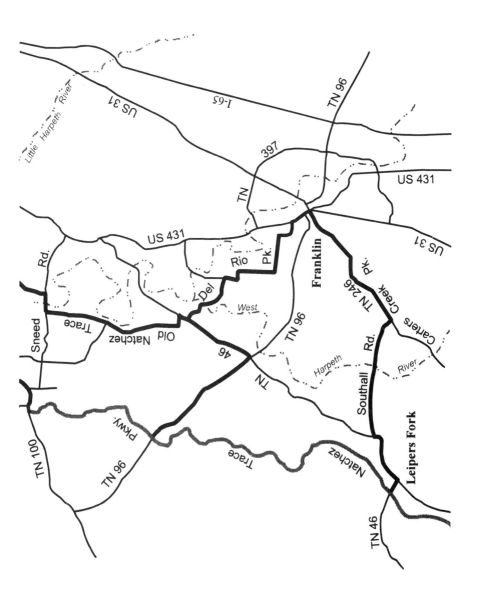

VICKSBURG TOUR

Distance: 237 miles
Starting Point: I-20 and Raymond-Clinton Rd. in Clinton (west of Jackson). See p. 137 for parking and airport access.
Terrain: Flat near Jackson, becoming moderately hilly between Vicksburg and Natchez.
Elev. Difference/Accumulated Climb: Day 1 - 250/910 ft.; Day 2 - 350/1,920 ft.; Day 3 - 300/1,590 ft.; Day 4 - 300/1,090 ft.; Day 5 - 220/1,080 ft.
Traffic: Moderate near Vicksburg and Natchez. Light on all other roads.
Camping: Vicksburg Battlefield Campground (end of Day 1—mile 35), Rocky Springs (Day 2—mile 25, Day 5—mile 13), Grand Gulf State Park (Day 2—mile 45), Natchez State Park/Traceway Campground (Day 3—mile 40, Day 4—mile 15).
Lodging: Vicksburg (end of Day 1—mile 35), Port Gibson (end of Day 2—mile 55, end of Day 4—mile 45), Canemount Plantation (Day 3—mile 13), Natchez (end of Day 3—mile 55), Church Hill (Day 4—mile 22), Mamie's Cottage (Day 5—mile 35).

The *Vicksburg Loop* takes you through the best of the Old South. Here you will pedal along roads previously trodden by General Grant's Union soldiers marching to Jackson and Vicksburg. Numerous antebellum homes still stand with all of the grace and grandeur from a *Gone with the Wind* scene. Most of these beautiful homes are in Vicksburg, Port Gibson, and Natchez, but several are nestled in the Mississippi countryside. You will also visit two townsites that have vanished with only a few traces of their existence remaining in the forest.

Your exact itinerary (and distances) will depend on whether you camp or stay in motels and B&Bs. Although these directions are for a five-day semi-loop route, some cyclists could finish in three days and others might prefer to take a week. Layover days in Vicksburg and Natchez are definitely worthwhile. Those desiring a shorter-distanced tour may easily return on the Natchez Trace from Rocky Springs or Port Gibson. I chose to start the tour near Jackson because of the airport and interstate access, but this trip could also be started at Natchez, Port Gibson, Vicksburg, or Rocky Springs. (See p.137 for airport and long term parking possibilities.) As you can see, you don't have to follow these directions exactly—tailor this trip to suit yourself!

Starting in Clinton, our tour heads west following Old US 80 and other rural roads through pastures, cotton fields, and forests. Union troops marched through this area en route to Vicksburg after capturing Jackson. A battle took place at Champion's Hill (also the name of one of the roads on this route) where General Grant repulsed a Confederate attack led by General Pemberton on May 16, 1863. Three days later the Battle of Vicksburg began.

In recent times, the rural towns of **Bolton** and **Edwards** have been largely forgotten when I-20 replaced US 80. After leaving Edwards, you soon pass Bonner Campbell College, a private college established in early 1800s that now serves as a Head Start Center for the underprivileged children living in the rural South. After a small descent, you pedal through flat cotton fields before crossing the Big Black River on an old truss bridge. This 300 mile long river once flowed through acres and acres of wetlands, most which have been drained for agriculture. The Natchez Trace avoided the swampy areas by staying on the ridges to the east of this river.

After a short steep climb out of the flood plain, our tour reaches **Vicksburg**, a friendly river town that was once referred to as the "key" to the Confederacy. President Lincoln wrote, "The war can never be brought to a close until that key is in our pocket." A tour of **Vicksburg National Military Park** will reveal how this "key" cost over 20,000 lives and made the citizens of the town suffer six weeks of constant bombardment during the siege. On July 4, 1863, General Pemberton had no choice but to surrender to end the starvation and destruction. (See p. 21 for an overview of the Civil War along the Natchez Trace.)

The battlefield, administered by the National Park Service, provides an enjoyable 15 mile loop (with short cut options) on one-way roads with light traffic. Cyclists and pedestrians may enter the park before gates open to auto traffic at 8:00 a.m. When we cycled through the grounds on a foggy April morning, the serenity of this area that once heard incessant gunfire and artillery, was an experience we will never forget. Not only does this ride give your mind something to think about, your legs will be equally engaged as you climb a total of 1,000 feet during this short loop. Numerous monuments, cannons, and interpretive markers are situated on the hilly terrain where Union and Confederate trenches can still be seen.

The remains of the Union ironclad gunboat *Cairo* were recovered from the Yazoo River near Vicksburg and pains-

Vicksburg National Military Park

takingly restored at the military park. In route to destroy Confederate batteries, the *Cairo* was the first vessel in history to strike an electrically detonated mine. An adjacent museum preserves artifacts from the boat, giving us a glimpse of life on one of these unique vessels.

With a dozen historic bed and breakfasts, numerous motels, and a campground, this town accommodates all types (and budgets) of bike tourists. Several motels, restaurants, and a private campground are conveniently located next to the battlefield. The B&Bs are found throughout the old part of town. B&B travelers may want to consider staying near Oak and Klein St. at one of the five historic inns overlooking the confluence of the Yazoo and Mississippi Rivers. Several locally owned eateries are within walking distance on Washington St.

Our visit to Vicksburg included a tour of the **McRaven Home**, which began as a pioneer cabin in 1797 and was expanded in 1836 and 1849 to the gracious Greek Revival home seen today. In addition to the rooms elegantly furnished with museum quality antiques, McRaven also displays scars from Union artillery fired over 100 years ago.

The bicycle provides a convenient way of touring the historic section of town as long as you avoid the busier streets. The visitor bureau, which you pass just before arriving at the Battlefield, provides a *Historic Driving Tour* map of the town's many attractions. This tour leads to everything from antebellum homes to the Coca-Cola museum where the beverage was first bottled. It also passes numerous shops, restaurants, and Hannah's Casino. On the next page is a modified version of the auto tour (to be used with *Historic Driving Tour* map) that avoids most of the busier streets.

Vicksburg Bike Tour
The following is a simplified (and mostly bike friendly)
tour of the town. The historic sites are in italics.

From the military park, bike toward town on Clay St.
(This short stretch is very busy.)
Right on Hope St. (first right) which becomes Grove
St. *Martha Vick House*
Right on Locust St. *Christ Church, Duff Green Man-*
sion B&B
Left on First East St. *Anchuca B&B*
Left on Cherry St. *Old Courthouse Museum, Toys and*
Soldiers Museum
Right on Grove St.
Left on Washington St. *Biedenharn Museum of Coca-*
Cola, Antique Doll and Toy Museum, Gray & Blue
Naval Museum, several restaurants.
Right on South St.
Left on Mulberry St. *The Corners B&B, Cedar Grove*
Mansion-Inn B&B
Right on Speed St. (Take right turns at every intersec-
tion till you are back at Speed St.) *Annabelle B&B,*
Floweree B&B, Belle of the Bends B&B
Left on Speed St. The *Stained Glass Manor* is located
to the right on Drummond St.
Left on Cherry St.
Right on South St. *The Balfour House B&B* is located
one block ahead on Crawford St.
Right on First North St./Court St. The *McRaven Tour*
Home is at the first left on Harrison St.
Left on Baldwyn Ferry Rd. after crossing RR tracks.
Right on Clay St. to return to the military park.

The directions for *Day 2* begin at the military park but if you are in the historic part of town, simply bike south on Cherry St. to Halls Ferry Rd. which connects with our route on Fisher Ferry Rd. Regardless of how you leave town, expect moderately busy roads including fast traffic on Fisher Ferry Rd. Within five miles or so, the traffic subsides. By the time you drop into the Big Black River flood plain, you'll be enjoying rural Mississippi on a peaceful country road.

After a substantial climb, a small country market awaits you at the intersection of Old Port Gibson Rd. For those camping, this is the last market before the campground at Grand Gulf State Park, and you may want to stock up in Vicksburg. The Natchez Trace Parkway is only one mile ahead at this intersection where our tour goes right on Old Port Gibson Rd. In approximately five miles you'll pass a small white church on the left. The Rocky Springs Church is the last remaining building of a town that once flourished in the plantation era. A short gravel path connects the church to the parking area of the Rocky Springs townsite which is part of the Natchez Trace Parkway.

The rest of *Day 2* follows the *Grand Gulf Loop* (see p. 173 for historical information) to **Grand Gulf Military Monument** following narrow canopied roads sunken deep into the Loess Soil. Camping is available at the Rocky Springs Site and at Grand Gulf Military Monument. Cyclists desiring motels or B&Bs will need to complete the *Day 2* route into Port Gibson. If you're short on time or energy, you can connect with the Parkway two miles south of the Rocky Springs Church for a more direct route to Port Gibson (see directions).

Day 3 leaves the beautiful historic homes of **Port Gibson** and follows the *Windsor Ruins Loop* (p. 170) to what was the grandest of the plantation homes. The Corinthian columns of the **Windsor Ruins** are all that remain today. Next you will pass the 1855 **Canemount Plantation**, now a B&B with a large nature/hunting preserve.

The remainder of *Day 3* uses the Natchez Trace Parkway all the way into Natchez. A fully restored stand and the second largest ceremonial Indian mound in the U.S. are the highlights before arriving in Natchez. (See p. 43 for historical and lodging information.) Camping opportunities are available near milepost 8 and 10.

Day 4 heads back to Emerald Mound. Just before reaching the Parkway, our route goes left on MS 553 and continues north on the *Church Hill Loop*. The community of **Church Hill** boasts a handful of gracious homes (one which is a B&B) situated on equally beautiful grounds. The oldest Episcopal church in Mississippi and the plantation where Andrew Jackson was married are also features of this tour.

The remainder of *Day 4* and most of *Day 5* return to Clinton on the Natchez Trace Parkway. Several historic sites and nature trails give you ample opportunity to rest your tush and stretch your legs.

Starting and Ending Your Tour

By Air: Unfortunately, the airport is on the east side of Jackson, and the Parkway is on the west. From what I have heard, there is no bike friendly way across town. Taxi service is available from the airport to the motels on Spring Ridge Rd. which is 2 miles away from the starting point.

Clinton Parking: If you spend at least one night at a motel in Clinton, you should be able to make parking arrangements at the motel for the duration of the tour. Even if you do not spend the night, some motels may allow you to park in their lot. It might be a good idea to offer to pay for parking priveleges in this situation.

North Jackson Parking: Another option (if traveling by car or plane) is to ship your bike to Indian Cycles (see *Jackson Bypass*) and have them assemble it. Several motels are also in the area if you need to spend the night. Overnight parking

may be available (with advance arrangements, call the headquarters at 662/680-4025 or 800/305-7417) at the Mississippi Crafts Center, the Clinton Visitor Center, or the Park
Service maintenance yard. B&Bs and motels are sometimes
able to arrange transportation (usually for a fee) to and from
the airport or the Trace. Refer to the *The Jackson Section* (p.
64) for lodging information.

Vicksburg Lodging
See Day 1 for lodging near the military park.

Annabelle B&B $$-$$$ (601/638-2000 or 800/791-2000) Elegant Victo-
rian Italianate home on river bluff. Features antiques, courtyard, pool, and
jacuzzi.
Anchuca B&B $$-$$$ (601/631-6800 or 800/469-2597) This 1830s
Greek Revival mansion features rooms furnished with period antiques,
pool, jacuzzi, and gardens.
Balfour House B&B $$-$$$ (601/638-7113 or 800/294-7113) This 1835
Greek Revival home was the Union headquarters after the siege. Rooms
furnished with antiques.
Belle of the Bends B&B $$-$$$ (601/634-0737 or 800/844-2308) This
Italianate home features antiques, rose garden, and a view of the river.
Cedar Grove Mansion B&B $$$ (601/636-1000 or 800/862-1300) Enjoy
river views along with 4 acres of gardens with fountains, gazebo, and pool.
Rooms furnished with antiques.
Cherry Street Cottages $$ (601/636-7086 or 800/636-7086) One of the
more economical B&Bs in town, the turn of the century Prairie-style home
is ideal for weary cyclists who just want to relax. Private cottages with
kitchen. Full breakfast included.
The Corners B&B $$-$$$ (601/636-7421 or 800/444-7421) Enjoy views
of the river from this unique 1873 home combining Greek and Victorian
architecture.
Duff Green Mansion B&B $$-$$$ (601/636-6968 or 800/992-0037) This
three story home (circa 1858) served as a hospital during the Civil War.
Features a large ballroom, gardens, and pool.
Relax Inn $ (601/631-0097) Nice downtown accommodations for those
on a budget.

Vicksburg Dining

Near the Battlefield:

Maxwell's—4207 Clay St. (Mon.-Fri. 11-10; Sat. lunch). Oysters, fresh seafood, and steaks.

Rowdy's—MS 27 and Clay St. (Daily 11-9:30) This local favorite has been serving fried and blackened catfish for over 50 years. Located one mile from the military park on busy Clay St.

Downtown Dining:

Andre's at Cedar Grove—2200 Oak St. (Dinner Tue.-Sun.) Enjoy a mint julep while listening to live piano music in a stately antebellum manion. Gourmet southern cuisine in elegant surroungings.

Borrello's—1306 Washington St. (daily 11-9) Italian cuisine specializing in fresh seafood

Daily Grind—1101 Washington St. (Mon.-Thurs. 11-5, dinner by reservation; Fri. & Sat. 11-10) Soups, salads, and sandwiches with entrees.

Duff's Tavern—1306 Washington St. (Daily 11-5) This elegant English Pub style manor serves grilled meats, fish, and pasta.

Walnut Hills—1214 Adam St. (Mon.-Fri. 11-9) Southern cooking, sandwiches, soups, salads.

STARTING POINT: This tour begins at the corner of Raymond-Clinton Rd. and the frontage road south of I-20 in Clinton (Exit 35 on I-20). Ask permission before leaving your car overnight at any location. See *Jackson Section* for more info. See p. 137 for parking and travel arrangements.

DAY 1
36 miles

Mile

0.0	From Raymond-Clinton Rd., bike west (away from Jackson) on Frontage Rd. (**Mkt, Rst, Ldg**—see *Jackson Bypass*, p. 64).
1.5	Go under the NTP.
3.8	**Mkt**
4.6	**Mkt**
5.7	Cross bridge over RR tracks.
8.4	**Left** on Raymond-Bolton Rd. (Airplane Rd.) (stop sign) (**Mkt**).
8.6	**Right** on Champion Hill Rd.
15.6	**Right** on Buck Reed Rd. (stop sign at the T-intersection).
15.7	**Left** on Cemetery Rd. after crossing the RR tracks.
17.6	**Left** on MS 467/Vicksburg St. (stop sign) (**Mkt, Rst, Ldg, Laundry**). Relax Inn $ (601/852-5116) is .5 mi. to the right near I-20.
18.0	Bear **right** on MS 467 (Vicksburg St.).
18.4	Continue straight on Old US 80 as MS 467 goes left. (There is a small **Supermkt** .8 mi. away on MS 467. Follow signs for MS 467 very carefully—there are two turns.)
18.7	Historic Bonner Campbell College, now a Head Start Center.
22.9	Cross Black River.
26.0	**Left** on Bovina Dr. after going under a bridge.
26.1	Cross RR tracks.
26.3	**Right** on Warriors Trail.
32.1	Cross MS 27 (stop sign)(**Mkt**).
32.6	Bear **right** on Old Hwy. 27 (stop sign).
35.2	Cross S. Frontage Rd., I-20, and N. Frontage Rd.

35.5   Vicksburg Tourist Information Center (**W, RR**).

35.6   End of *Day 1* at Vicksburg National Military Park (**Mkt, Rst, Ldg, Cpg**). Go right on Clay St. to reach the EconoLodge $ (601/634-8766 or 800/533-2666) and the Hampton Inn $$ (601/636-6100 or 800/HAMPTON). Go right on Clay St., then left on Frontage Rd. to reach the Motel 6 $ (601/638-5077 or 800/466-8356), the Battlefield Inn $ (601/638-5811 or 800/359-9363) and the Vicksburg Battlefield Campground (private, 601/636-2025) (showers, laundry). See suggested route on p. 135 to reach B&Bs and restaurants in downtown. Maps are available at the tourist information center.

DAY 2
55 miles

If you are starting in downtown, go south on Cherry St. and continue on Halls Ferry Rd. to Fisher Ferry Rd.

0.0   From Vicksburg National Military Park, cross Clay St. and continue on Old Hwy. 27.

0.4   **Right** on South Frontage Rd.

0.5   **Left** on Porters Chapel Rd.

4.3   **Right** on Halls Ferry Rd. (stop sign at the T-intersection).

4.5   **Left** on Fisher Ferry Rd. (stop sign at the T-intersection) (**Supermkt**).

7.4   Bear **left** at the top of the hill where Grange Hall Rd. goes right (**Mkt**).

9.3   **Mkt**

17.7   Cross Big Black River.

18.9   **Right** on Old Port Gibson Rd. (4-way stop) (**Mkt**).

25.5   Rocky Springs Church. A short path leads to the parking area of this Parkway historic site.

27.3   Road to left connects with Natchez Trace.

32.7   **Right** on Willows Rd. at the 5-way intersection.

35.7   **Left** on US 61 (stop sign).

36.2   **Right** on Ingleside/Karnack Ferry Rd. (also known as Old Grand Gulf Rd.)

38.1	**Right** on Karnack Ferry Rd.(YMCA Rd./Old Grand Gulf Rd.)(stop sign).
39.6	**Left** on Y-Camp Rd.
41.2	**Right** on Back Grand Gulf Rd. (first right).
43.5	**Right** (staying on Back Grand Gulf Rd.) at the next intersection.
44.5	**Right** at the bottom of a steep hill.
44.6	**Left** on Main Grand Gulf Rd. at the next intersection. The site of Ft. Cobun and views of the Mississippi River are .7 mi. to the right.
44.8	Grand Gulf State Park (**W, RR, PS, Cpg**). This small park has picnic shelters and a campground with hot showers.
46.8	**Right** on Bald Hill Rd. near the Grand Gulf Nuclear Power Station.
52.1	**Right** on Oil Mill Rd. (stop sign at the T-intersection) and cross Bayou Pierre. Road becomes Anthony St. in Port Gibson.
54.5	**Right** on Flower St. after passing oil refinery.
54.7	**Left** on Carol St.
54.9	End of *Day 2* in Port Gibson at US 61/Church St. (**Supermkt, Rst, Ldg, Laundry**). See p. 63 for lodging and dining information.

DAY 3

55 miles

See Windsor Ruins Loop for map

0.0	From Church St./US 61, bike west on Carol St.
0.2	Bear **left** as you leave town. Road becomes Rodney Rd. and later MS 552.
4.2	Pt. Lookout
10.3	Windsor Ruins
14.4	**Mkt, Rst**—Located 1/2 mile to the right near the entrance to Alcorn University. You may continue through the campus and rejoin MS 552.
20.2	**Right** on the access road to the NTP.
20.3	**Left** on the NTP going south. See p. 60 for historic sites and services.

50.7   **Right** on Liberty Rd. at the SouthernTerminus and continue into Natchez (**Mkt, Ldg, Cpg**). See Natchez Chapter (p. 43) for details.

53.0   End of *Day 3* in Natchez.

DAY 4
40 miles
See Church Hill Loop for map

0.0   Bike back to the Trace and bike north to Emerald Mound at mp 10.3. *Milage starts at Southern Terminus.*

10.3   **Left** at Emerald Mound/MS553.

10.4   **Right** on MS 553 where the road to Emerald Mound goes straight.

16.6   Enter Church Hill Community (**Ldg**). Historic homes. Jim's Cabin Rental $$ (601/442-1456).

16.9   Christ Church, Wagner's Store.

21.4   Springfield Plantation. (Tours available 601/786-3802.)

22.4   **Left** on NTP access road.

22.6   **Right** on NTP going north. See p. 60 for historic sites and services.

39.9   End of *Day 4* at Port Gibson. Use US 61 exit (mp 37.5) and follow northbound *Port Gibson Optional Detour* on p. 62. (**Supermkt, Rst, Ldg, Laundry**). Campers should continue on NTP to Rocky Springs at mp 52.4.

DAY 5
48 miles

0.0   From MS 18 in Port Gibson, continue north on the NTP. See p. 61 for historic sites and services.

47.7   Exit onto Pinehaven Rd. at mp 89.0 (**W, RR, Mkt**) Starting point is 2 miles away. See *Jackson Section* for map.

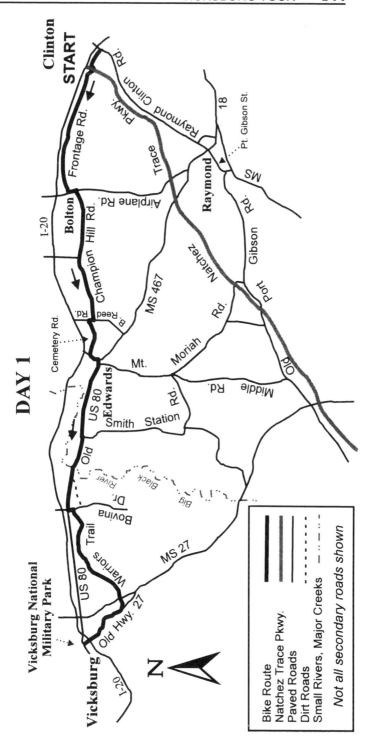

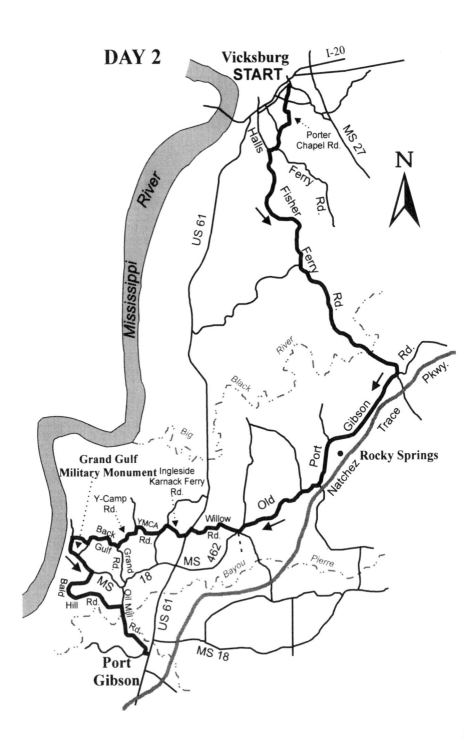

DAY 2

TENNESSEE RIVER TOUR

Distance: 171-210 miles
Starting Point: Meriwether Lewis Site (mp 386)
Terrain: Very steep hills east of the TN River with flat-to-rolling stretches in between. Flatter terrain west of the river.
Elev. Difference/Accumulated Climb: 600/5,000-6,000 ft.
Traffic: Moderate traffic on TN 20, TN 13, TN 57, TN 128 at Pickwick Dam, and CR 14 between Waterloo and the NTP. None of these moderately busy stretches are longer than 6 miles. Light on all other roads.
Camping: Crazy Horse Park (Day 1/Option 1—mile 22), Clifton Marina (end of Day 1—mile 40 or 53), Battlefield Campground (Day 2—mile 43), Pickwick Landing State Park (end of Day 2—mile 57), Pickwick Dam (Day 3—mile 2), Burtons Branch (Day 3-mile 8), Waterloo (Day 3/Option 2—mile 26), Brush Creek (Day 3/Option 2—mile 31), Colbert Ferry (end of Day 3/Option 2—mile 41).
Lodging: Crazy Horse Park Cabins (Day 1/Option 1—mile 22), Waynesboro (Day 1/Option 2—mile 35), Clifton (end of Day 1—mile 40 or 53), Savannah (Day 2—mile 32 or 38 plus 8 or 4 add'l mi.), Counce (Day 2—mile 56), Pickwick Landing State Park (end of Day 2—mile 57), Florence (Day 3/Option 2—mile 40 plus 17 add'l mi. or shuttle from Limestone Manor B&B).

This three to four day journey takes you over the wooded ridges of the western Highland Rim and down along clear cascading creeks that have carved lovely valleys in this hilly region. The rim occasionally reaches 1,000 feet in elevation, nearly 600 feet above the Tennessee River. Need I tell you to expect to do some climbing on this ride?

In May of 1993, Ann and I embarked on a three-day excursion from the Meriwether Lewis Site to Tishomingo State Park after which we headed west on MS 25 to Pickwick

State Park. Boy, was that a mistake! MS 25 was nothing less than a constant stream of speeding logging trucks on a narrow highway. From Savannah, though, our trip back was absolutely delightful with gorgeous scenery and peaceful roads. After surviving the logging trucks, we didn't mind the hilly terrain one bit.

I have altered the *Tennessee River Tour* from our original tour replacing MS 25 with a network of lightly traveled rural roads used only occasionally by trucks. With several camping and lodging possibilities, the daily distances and number of days can easily be changed to suit yourself. When planning distances, keep in mind that the terrain is very hilly east of the Tennessee River!

Shortly after leaving the Meriwether Lewis Site, our route reaches **Hohenwald**, originally a Swiss-German settlement established in the 1870s. Hohenwald, which means high forests, became known for it artists and craftsmen. Numerous shops and restaurants are located in the center of town (go right on TN 48 where our route goes left). Another worthwhile stop is the **Lewis County Museum of Natural History** which contains an extensive collection of exotic animals from around the world and local historical artifacts including items belonging to Meriwether Lewis.

From Hohenwald, you can reach the first day's destination via two routes. The shorter route crosses the **Buffalo River** where the Crazy Horse Campground and Canoe Livery is located. If you aren't in a hurry, consider taking a few hours to paddle one of the most beautiful and unspoiled rivers in Middle Tennessee. After cycling back to the rim, a fast descent brings you into the lovely Beech Creek Valley.

Option 2 follows TN 99 as it winds through the peaceful Buffalo Valley. Canoeing and camping are also available along this route. Expect some challenging hills along with light traffic and miles of hardwood forests. **Waynesboro** makes an excellent lunch stop with two restaurants on the town square. From here, the Clifton Turnpike takes you through the Eagle Creek Wildlife Management Area to the tiny town of Clifton.

When we pedaled into **Clifton** with its one block Main St., we felt as if we had gone 60 years back in time. Established along the Tennessee River in early 1800s, the town quickly grew as a port during the steamboat era. We were also delighted to discover a vegetarian restaurant, a rarity in rural Tennessee, but it is no longer in business. Southern cookin', catfish, and pizza ought to satisfy your hunger.

On *Day 2*, our route originally crossed the river at Clifton on a small ferry that has been replaced (alas!) by a new bridge south of town. Should you desire an old fashioned ferry crossing, continue south on TN 128 rather than going west on TN 114. Turn right on Saltillo Ferry Rd. and join the *Day 2* route in Saltillo. If you opt to do this, you will bypass some excellent cycling roads that wind through the sparsely populated countryside west of the river. Most of *Day 2* uses the "Cycling the River" route established by the Tennessee Department of Transportation (see *Appendices*).

You might want to consider a short detour to spend the night in **Savannah**, a friendly town with an active bike club. The "Ride the River" held on the last Saturday each April brings cyclists from all over the mid-South to experience the miles of wonderful cycling roads on either side of the river. The White Elephant B&B along with several motels and restaurants show off this town's hospitality.

Founded in 1830 after the Chickasaws and Cherokees were forced to leave their hunting grounds for Oklahoma, Savannah quickly became an important river port. Today, the town hosts numerous restaurants, shops, and the Tennessee River Museum adjacent to the courthouse. The museum boasts an impressive exhibit of fossils and exhibits on the geological history of the area. Many Indian artifacts are displayed including one of the best stone-effigy pipes ever recovered. The Civil War is well represented with over 100 types of bullets from nearby Shiloh, a reproduction of the *USS Cairo*, and many other relics of the war. From here, you can begin the two-mile Historic Trail which showcases several homes and sites of this river town.

Next our route travels through **Shiloh National Military Park**, a crucial battle site in the western campaign of the Civil War. In April of 1862, the Union Army under General U.S. Grant had set camp near a country church called Shiloh, meaning "place of peace" in Hebrew. Sadly, it is ironic that this site became one of the bloodiest battles of the Civil War, with 13,000 Union casualties and 11,000 Confederate losses.

At dawn on April 6, Confederate General Johnston's 44,000 troops surprised the Union encampment. Johnston hoped to destroy Grant's Army of the Tennessee before they were reinforced by General Buell's Army of the Ohio. The Union troops retreated, but eventually managed to hold a line above Pittsburg Landing. General Johnston was killed and General Beauregard took over the Confederate command. With Confederate victory in grasp, Beauregard fell back. The fighting continued the next day but Buell's forces had joined Grant's, and the Confederates retreated to Corinth Mississippi.

Today, a nine-mile paved loop tour takes visitors to various sites of the battle including a large Union cemetery and a mass Confederate gravesite. A visitor center and historical markers along the roads give the history of the battle. While cycling the peaceful roads and enjoying the tranquil scenery, it is hard to imagine the nearly 100,000 soldiers struggling to survive in these fields and forests. Don't get too lost in thought because the route between TN 22 and TN 57 requires careful navigation!

Leaving Shiloh, you'll continue to enjoy quiet backroads before heading to Pickwick Landing on moderately busy TN 57 which passes a large pulp mill (picnic sites and an arboretum of native tress are open to the public). The entrance to **Pickwick State Park**, just beyond the TN 128 junction, offers camping, lodging, hiking, swimming, dining, and fishing.

Day 3 begins by crossing **Pickwick Dam** which provides over 50 miles of slack water along the Tennessee River. But what may be more important to the local people is water recreation. It seems almost everyone here has a boat, and the markets sell more bait than beer and chewing tobacco. The Tennessee Valley Authority operates a visitor center and museum at the dam.

Day 3 gives you the option of returning to Meriwether Lewis or spending another night out in Alabama. The first option meanders through beautiful countryside on quiet roads before joining the Natchez Trace at Collinwood.

Boldly facing the artillery at Shiloh Military Park

The second option follows Holland Creek Rd. for a rural treat of a ride into **Waterloo**, Alabama. The Main St. (a half mile off the route) consists of a bank, post office, BBQ restaurant, a gas station/market, and a small museum in a beautiful 120 year old home. This sleepy forgotten town founded in 1819 was once an important port on the river. During the steamboat era, large boats would unload goods and passengers here and transfer them to smaller vessels for the journey to the foot of Muscle Shoals. Thousands of Native Americans boarded vessels in Waterloo during the Trail of Tears in the 1830s.

Union gunboats attacked Waterloo in 1862, and General W.T. Sherman made headquarters here before crossing the Tennessee River in 1863. From Waterloo, AL 14 follows the edge of the Pickwick Lake, affording wonderful views of the forested banks on the other side.

Just before joining the Natchez Trace, our route passes a little spring known as Gravelly Spring. In 1865, Major General J.H. Wilson assembled the largest cavalry force ever amassed in the western hemisphere. 22,000 Union troops camped and trained between here and Waterloo. We can only imagine what it must have smelled like... Wilson's cavalry later burned the University of Alabama at Tusculoosa and captured Jefferson Davis.

After joining the Natchez Trace, this option continues to the primitive cyclists-only campsite at Colbert Ferry. Lodging is available in Florence, and camping (with showers,) cabins, and a historic hotel are 25 miles south at the Tishomingo exit.

STARTING POINT: Meriwether Lewis Historic Site (mm 385.9). This ride begins at the log cabin visitor center. Call the Park Service at 662/680-4025 before overnight parking here.

DAY 1
40 or 52 miles

Mile

0.0   Turn **right** from parking area and follow signs to TN 20.

0.3   **Right** on TN 20 toward Hohenwald (stop sign at the T-intersection).
       Go to Option 1 or Option 2

Option 1

6.2   **Mkt**

6.4   **Left** on TN 48 South at the traffic light (**Mkt, Supermkt, Rst, Ldg**). All services (see p. 106) to the right on TN 48 in Hohenwald.

20.7   **Left** on TN 13 (stop sign at the T-intersection)(**Mkt**).

22.4   Cross the Buffalo River (**Mkt, Ldg, Cpg**). Crazy Horse Park (931/722-5213 or 800/722-5213) offers lodging, camping (showers) and also rents canoes.

24.7   **Rst**

26.3   **Right** on TN 228/Beech Creek Rd.

29.1   **Mkt**

32.5   **Left** on TN 228 (now Morrison Creek Rd.) where Beech Creek Rd. goes straight.

37.4   **Left** on TN 128.

38.0   Bear Inn Golf Resort (**Ldg, Rst**) (931/676-5552)

38.8   Clifton Park with tables and picnic shelter overlooking river.

39.5   End of *Day 1* at Main St. in Clifton (**Mkt, Supermkt, Rst, Ldg, Cpg**). Clifton Motel $ (931/676-3515), Pillow St. B&B $$ (931/676-3425), Clifton Marina and Campground (no showers) (931/676-5225).

Option 2

6.1   **Left** on TN 99 West (really south) and make another **left** (still TN 99) a few yards later (**Mkt**).

12.5   Cross Buffalo River.

17.7   **Left**, staying on TN 99, at stop sign.

18.3   **Right**, staying on TN 99.

20.2   **Cpg**. Buffalo Valley Canoeing (931/796-5596 or 800/339-5596) (showers).

32.3   **Right**, staying on TN 99.

35.0   **Right** on US 64 (traffic light).

35.5   **Rst, Supermkt.**

35.7   Straight onto Dexter Woods Memorail Blvd. at the traffic light.

36.3   Do a 1/2 circle around the courthouse in Waynesboro and go **right** on High St. (Old US 64) going west (**Rst, Ldg**). Ren-Cass Motel $ (931/722-7733).

36.5   **Right** on Clifton Turnpike (easy to miss).

37.8   Cross US 64 bypass.

50.3   **Right** on TN 114 (stop sign at the T-intersection).

51.3   **Right** on Main St.

52.3   End of *Day 1* at TN 128 in Clifton (see *Option 1* for services).

DAY 2
58 miles

0.0   From Main St., bike south on TN 128.

0.4   **Right**, staying onTN 128, at T-stop.

0.9   Clifton Marina and Campground (see end of *Day 1*).

1.6   **Right** on TN 114/128 going west (stop sign at the T-intersection).

2.9   Straight on TN 114 as TN 128 goes left. Optional route to Savannah.

5.8   Cross Tennessee River.

7.0   **Left** on TN 114.

10.4   **Left** on TN 69/114 going south.

11.2   Straight onto TN 69.

21.0   **Left** on Main St. in Saltillo (**Mkt, Rst**). Rst is toward river (east) on Main St.

21.1	**Right** on Oak Ave. (first right). Oak Ave. becomes Saltillo Rd.
27.9	Bear **left** on Glendale Rd. where Marshall Rd. goes straight.
32.4	Cross Coffee Landing Rd. (stop sign). Savannah (**Supermkt, Rst, Ldg**) is 6 mi. away by going left at this intersection, then left again on US 64. Savannah Motel $ (731/925-3392) Savannah Lodge $ (731/925-8586). Call tourism office (800/552-FUNN) for add'l lodging.
33.5	**Left**, staying on Glendale Rd., where Old Union Rd. goes straight.
36.5	**Left** on TN 69 (stop sign at the T-intersection).
38.1	**Left** on US 64 in the town of Crump (stop sign) (**Ldg**). River Heights Motel $ (731/632-4535).
38.2	**Right** on TN 22 (**Mkt, Rst**). Savannah (see above for services) is 4 mi. east on US 64 (fast traffic.)
43.3	**Left** on Pittsburg Landing Rd. (Grant Rd.) at Shiloh National Military Park (**Rst, Cpg**). The Battlefield Campground (731/689-3098, showers) is 3 mi. ahead on TN 20.
44.3	**Right** at the stop sign at the bookstore and visitor center (**W, RR**). Map available at visitor center.
44.4	**Right** on Corinth-Pittsburg Landing Rd. (Confederate Dr.) at the next stop sign and follow the Battlefield Tour.
45.7	**Left** on Hamburg-Savannah Rd. (Johnston Rd.) at the X-style 4-way intersection. To continue the battlefield tour, go straight and follow signs. Turn right (discontinue the tour) on Hamburg-Savannah Rd. in 5.2 mi. This will add 4 miles to your trip.
46.4	Straight at stop sign.
47.6	Park boundary. The county road you are now on is called Federal Rd.
49.7	Bear **left** on Leath Rd. at the Y where Federal Rd. goes to the right.
51.6	Bear **right** (staying on Leath Rd.) near the large powerlines.
53.6	**Left** on TN 57 (stop sign).

56.7	Town of Counce (**Mkt, Supermkt, Rst, Ldg**). Little Andy's Sportsman Lodge & Cabins $ (731/689-3750).
57.7	Straight on TN 57 where TN 128 goes left.
57.8	End of *Day 2* at Pickwick Landing State Park (**Rst, Cpg, Ldg**). Campground (showers), inn, and cabins are 1-3 mi. from entrance. $$ (731/689-3135).

DAY 3
41 or 74 miles

0.0	From TN 57, bike north on TN 128.
0.8	Cross Pickwick Lake.
1.7	TVA Damsite Campground (**Cpg**—showers).
2.1	**Mkt**
2.5	**Right** on Worley Rd. (easy to miss).
3.0	**Right** on Pyburns Rd. (stop sign).
8.1	Straight at the 4-stop. (**Mkt, Cpg**). Burtons Branch Campground (no showers) is 2.5 mi. to the right (south).
9.2	**Right** on TN 69 (stop sign at the T-intersection).

Go to Option 1 or Option 2

Option 1

11.7	**Mkt**
12.7	**Left** on Cherry Chapel Lp.
18.9	**Left** on Number 2 Rd. (easy to miss).
22.9	**Left** on Gillis Rd. at the T-intersection (**Mkt**).
23.3	**Right** on TN 203 (stop sign at the T-intersection).
28.5	**Mkt**
29.3	**Right**, staying on TN 203, at stop sign.
35.5	**Mkt**
40.8	**Left** on TN 13. (Note: You can walk your bike onto the Parkway at the fire tower by the cemetery.)
42.9	**Right** on TN 13/Broadway in Collinwood (traffic light) (**Supermkt, Rst, Cpg, PS**). Cyclists may camp at city park. Showers at visitors center.
43.0	Continue straight where TN 13 goes left.

43.1   **Left** on the NTP access road.

43.2   **Left** on NTP going north. See p. 105 for historic sites and services.

74.2   End of tour at Meriwether Lewis Site!

Option 2

11.5   **Right** on Holland Creek Rd.

12.8   Bear **left** (staying Holland Cr. Rd.) at the yield sign where McKelvey Hollow Rd. goes right.

19.1   Road becomes CR 14 in Alabama.

25.5   Hart Campground. (**Cpg**—laundry, showers) (256/768-1555).

26.1   **Left** (staying on CR 14) at the stop sign. **Mkt** and **Rst** are .4 mi. to right in Waterloo at this intersection.

30.6   Brush Creek County Park (**W**, **RR**, **PS**, **Mkt**, **Rst**, **Cpg**). No showers.

36.5   **Left** on NTP on-ramp. Florence (**Rst**, **Ldg**) is 15 miles east. See *Florence Loop* for possible routes. Call **888/FLO-TOUR** for lodging.

36.7   **Right** on NTP going south.

41.3   End of *Day 3* at Colbert Ferry (**W**, **RR**, **Cpg**—cyclists only, no showers. See p. 99 for directions). Cherokee (**Supermkt**, **Rst**) is 6 mi. south. Camping (showers) and lodging also available 25 mi. south at the Tishomingo exit. See p. 98 for accommodations.

DAY 4

59 miles

0.0   From Colbert Ferry, bike north on the NTP. See p. 104 for historic sites and services.

58.6   End of tour at Meriwether Lewis Site!

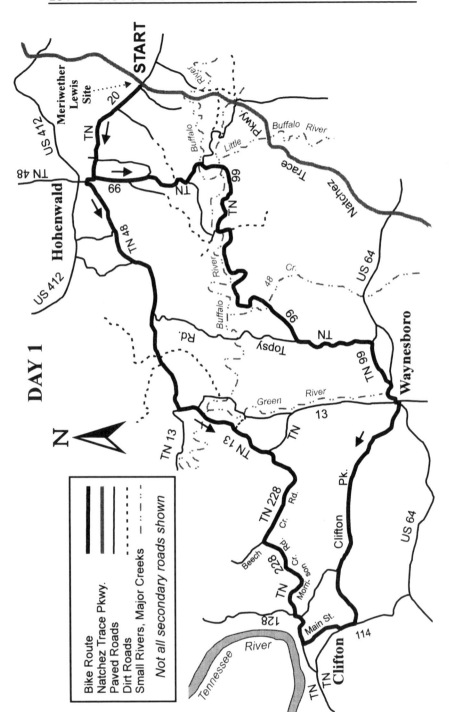

DAY 2

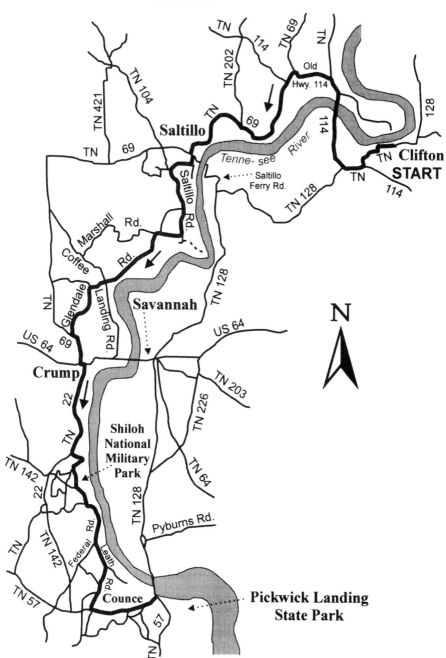

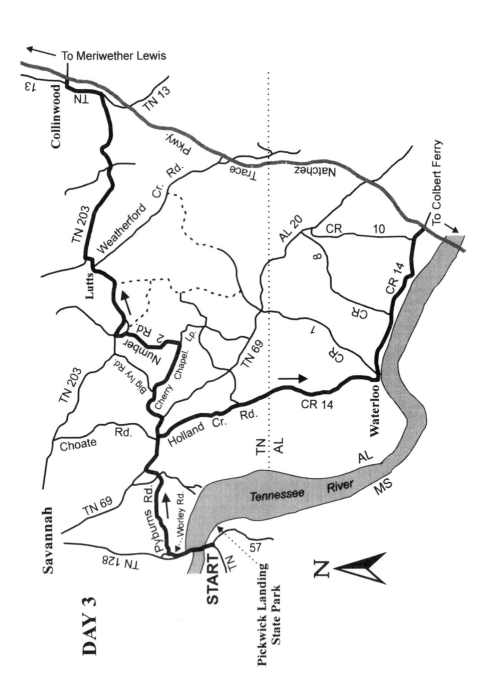

SNOW CREEK TOUR

Distance: 115-125 miles
Starting Point: Franklin, TN
Terrain: Rolling to hilly with a few very steep climbs.
Elev. Difference/Accumulated Climb: 470/3,050 ft.
Traffic: Moderately busy near Franklin and light to moderate on TN 50. Moderate to heavy traffic on TN 96 (wide paved shoulders). Light on all other roads.
Camping: TN 50 & NTP (Day 1—mile 32, Day 2—mile 22 or 32), Fall Hollow (Day 1—mile 48), Meriwether Lewis Site (end of Day 1—mile 54).
Lodging: Water Valley B&B (Day 1—mile 23, Day 2—mile 30 or mile 40), US 412 (Day 1—mile 48), TN 46/Leipers Fork (Day 2—mile 43 or 53), Franklin (end of Day 2—mile 61 or 71).

Whether you are looking for a challenging single day century or a relaxed three day excursion, you will enjoy cycling through this region of green pastures, old barns, and steep forested hillsides carved by clear tumbling creeks. Several antebellum plantation homes are found in the countryside and in Franklin. While the beauty of Middle Tennessee is impressive, so are its hills! The climbs rarely exceed one mile but they are steep. Unless you are strong rider with a light racing bike, a triple chain ring is a must.

Several B&Bs, a simple motel, and three camping areas provide accommodations for all types of overnight touring. You can easily tailor this tour to fit your own time schedule and distances desired. The *Snow Creek Tour* may be combined with the *Tennessee River Tour* for a week of great cycling.

If you are driving a car to Franklin, you will need to find your own parking location. Transportation can be arranged from the Nashville airport as well (see p. 38). Another option is to start and end the tour at the ranger station in Leipers Fork (call 662/680-4025 for parking permission). To begin the tour from here, bike east on Southall Rd., go right on Carl Rd., then right on TN 246, and you are on the route for *Day 1.* Your milages will only be .3-.5 mile higher. This route bypasses Franklin and shaves 15 miles off the entire tour.

This tour included here embarks from **Franklin**, a cyclist's heaven complete with bakery, ice cream store, fruit stand, drug store soda fountain, and several good restaurants, all wrapped in a well-preserved small town atmosphere. The town, founded in 1799, is listed in the National Register of Historic Places. The Masonic Hall (1823) on Second Ave. was the first three-story building in the state (and possibly west of the Allegheny Mountains) and was also the location of an important meeting between Andrew Jackson and Chickasaw chiefs. The Battle of Franklin was significant in the Civil War, with 8,000 Union and Confederate soldiers losing their lives in November of 1864. Twice, Ann and I escorted Adventure Cycling Tours to the Carter House that stood in the heart of the battle. After picnicking, we walked the grounds, viewing the bullet holes still in the house and outbuildings.

Heading west from Franklin, the traffic gradually subsides as cows and horses become more numerous than cars. After passing the tiny community of Burwood, Carters Creek Pike begins a relatively easy ascent of the Tennessee Valley Divide. After turning onto TN 247, a very tough hill awaits as you head up to Theta after which a very fast (and dangerous if you don't brake) descent takes you into the Snow Creek Valley. Several lovely old white farmhouses overlook the pastures and corn fields of this valley.

After climbing a less severe hill on TN 50, our route joins the Trace where you have several options. You may prefer to call it quits and camp at the trailhead on TN 50. Restrooms are nearby at the **Gordon Site** on the Parkway, and a market/deli is just west on TN 50. For those desiring more luxurious accommodations (plus a tasty breakfast in the morning) the Water Valley B&B can be reached from the town of Santa Fe or the TN 7 exit on the Trace. Day riders desiring to accomplish the honest century should go south to the Swan View Overlook before returning north on the Trace.

The directions included here continue south on the Trace to the campground at the **Meriwether Lewis Site**. For lodging or camping with showers, exit at US 412 and spend the night at the Ridgetop B&B or Fall Hollow Campground. Another option is pedal west for 6 miles on US 412 to the Deerfield Inn in the Swiss-German town of **Hohenwald**.

For a truly unique overnight stay, extend your journey to **The Farm**, a vegetarian co-op founded by philosopher Steve Gaskin. Here you will find camping with solar showers, hostel-type accommodations, and a bargain-priced B&B. Allow time for a hike along a beautiful creek to an enticing swimming hole. To reach The Farm:
Take US 412 east for 3 miles
Right on Swan Creek Rd. (easy to miss) and continue for 6.5 miles (including a big hill).
Left on TN 20 (stop sign) and continue for 2.6 miles.
Left on Drake Ln. (easy to miss) and continue for 3 miles.
Left on entrance road to The Farm (not well marked.)

The second day (which may be your third or fourth) heads north on the Trace to the infamous **TN 96 bridge** and then continues east to Franklin on the wide-shouldered TN 96. *Option 2* replaces a section of the Parkway between US 412 and TN 50 that you will have already pedaled with a delightful excursion through the **Swan Creek Valley**. Should you desire to reduce your daily distances, spend the night in **Leipers Fork**. From this community, there are several excellent day rides (see the *Backbone Ridge Loop*, *Fernvale Loop*, and *Leipers Creek Loop*) that can be cycled in half a day.

STARTING POINT: Franklin, TN. If driving, you will need to find your own parking location.

DAY 1
54 miles

Mile

0.0   From downtown Franklin (5th and Main St.), bike west on W. Main St. which becomes Carters Creek Pk./TN 246.

4.0   Continue straight on TN 246 at Southall Rd. (**Mkt**).

11.0   Burwood Community (**Mkt**).

14.1   **Right** on TN 247.

16.4   **Mkt**

23.0   Cross TN 7 (**Mkt, Rst, Ldg**). Water Valley B&B $$$ (931/682-2266) is 5 mi. away on Option 2 of *Leipers Creek Loop*.

29.3   **Right** on TN 50 (stop sign at the T-intersection).

32.3   Go south on the Natchez Trace Pkwy. (**Mkt, Ldg, Cpg**). See p. 112 for historic sites and services. A market, fairly well stocked with canned and dry goods plus deli, is 1 mi. west on TN 50. A cyclists-only camp area is located at the trailhead just west of the NTP. Restrooms and picnic shelter available .5 mi. south on NTP.

48.3   TN 412 (**Mkt, Rst, Ldg**). Fall Hollow Campground (not yet open at the time of publication), located at the Parkway exit, offers camping (showers) lodging, and a market. Ridgetop B&B (931/285-2777 or 800/377-2770) is located 4 mi. east. The Deerfield Inn (931/796-1500) is 6 mi. west of the Parkway in the town of Hohenwald. The Farm (B&B, hostel, and campground with showers) is 18 mi. away. (Advance arrangements required, 931/964-3574, see p. 162 for directions).

53.5   End of *Day 1* at TN 20/Meriwether Lewis Historic Site (**Mkt, Cpg**) The Parkway campground (no showers) is 2 mi. away. A market with a fair selection of canned and packaged goods is 1.7 mi. east of the Parkway on TN 20.

DAY 2
61 or 71 miles

Option 1

0.0	From the Meriwether Lewis Site, bike north on the Parkway toward Nashville. (See p. 111 for historic sites and services.)
22.1	TN 50 (mp 408) (**Mkt, Cpg**).
29.8	TN 7 (mp 416) (**Mkt, Ldg**)
43.1	Leipers Fork/TN 46 (mp 429)(**Mkt, Rst, Ldg**).
51.5	Exit onto TN 96 at mp 437.4.
52.1	**Right** on TN 96 going east.
60.5	**Right** on US 431/5th Ave (traffic light).
60.6	End of tour at Main St. in Franklin!

Option 2

0.0	From the Meriwether Lewis Site, bike north on the Parkway toward Nashville.
5.2	Exit onto US 412 at mp 391.1
5.4	**Left** on US 412 at the end of the access road (**Mkt**).
7.7	**Right** on Salem Rd. (becomes Swan Creek Rd.)
20.7	**Right** on TN 50 (stop sign).
31.4	**Mkt**
32.4	**Left** on NTP access road (**Cpg**). See p. 112 for historic sites and services.
32.6	**Right** on the NTP going north.
39.8	TN 7 (mp 416) (**Mkt, Ldg**)
53.1	Leipers Fork/TN 46 (mp 429)(**Mkt, Rst, Ldg**).
61.5	Exit onto TN 96 at mp 437.4.
62.1	**Right** on TN 96 going east.
70.5	**Right** on US 431/5th Ave (traffic light).
70.6	End of tour at Main St. in Franklin!

DAY 1 & 2
NORTHERN SECTION

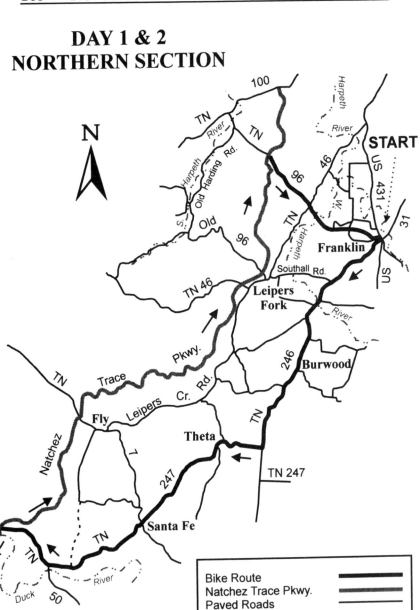

Bike Route
Natchez Trace Pkwy.
Paved Roads
Dirt Roads
Small Rivers, Major Creeks

Not all secondary roads shown

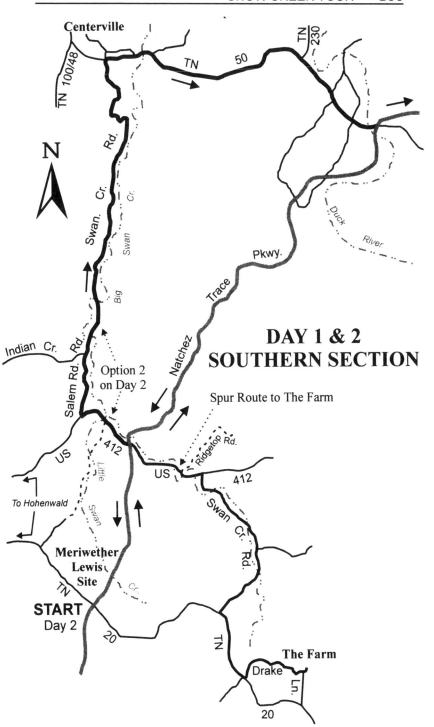

Centerville

TN 100/48

TN   50   TN 230

N

Swan. Cr. Rd.

Big Swan Cr.

Duck River

Pkwy.

Trace

Natchez

Indian Cr.

Salem Rd. Rd.

Option 2 on Day 2

**DAY 1 & 2
SOUTHERN SECTION**

Spur Route to The Farm

Ridgetop Rd.

US   412

US   412

Little Swan

To Hohenwald

Swan Cr. Rd.

**Meriwether
Lewis
Site**

Cr.

TN

START
Day 2   20

TN

The Farm

Drake   Ln.

20

CHURCH HILL LOOP

Distance: 22 miles
Starting Point: Mt. Locust Visitor Center (mp 15.5)
Terrain: Flat to moderately hilly.
Elev. Difference/Accumulated Climb: 280/620 ft.
Traffic: Light on all roads.
Combining Rides: *Windsor Ruins Loop* (10 miles to
the north on NTP), *Vicksburg Tour.*

This simple excursion offers an abundance of historical
sights for a short bike ride. Beginning at Mt. Locust, the only
restored stand on the Trace, the *Church Hill Loop* heads
south to Emerald Mound which is the second largest ceremonial mound in the Southeast.

After leaving the Trace, this route follows MS 553 to
the Church Hill community which features three historic
homes. The Christ Church, the oldest Episcopal church in
the state (circa 1790), sits proudly on top of the hill for which
this community is named. Across the street is one of the few
classic country stores remaining in the rural south.

The last stop before returning to the Trace is the Springfield Plantation (circa 1784) which is the oldest columned
two-story home west of the Atlantic seaboard. In 1791 (37
years before his presidency), Andrew Jackson traveled to
Springfield to marry his beloved Rachel Robards. At the
time, they were both unaware that her divorce from her first
husband was not technically complete, and this became a
political issue that would plague the Jacksons for the rest of
their lives. American politics hasn't changed!

Heading back to Mt. Locust, local cyclists always look
forward to the section where towering pines line the Parkway offering some reprieve from the relentless summer sun.

Christ Church in Church Hill

STARTING POINT: Mt. Locust Visitor Center (mp 15.5)

Mile

0.0   Bike south on the NTP toward Natchez.

5.3   **Right** on MS 553 at the Emerald Mound exit (mp 10.3).

5.4   Bear **right** on MS 553 where the road to Emerald Mound goes straight ahead.

11.6   Enter Church Hill Community. Logonia, Cedars, and Oak Grove historic homes.

11.9   Christ Church, Wagner's Store (**Ldg**) Jim's Cabin Rental $$ (601/442-1456).

16.4   Springfield Plantation (.6 mi. roundtrip on dirt road). Tours available, 601/786-3802.

17.4   **Left** on NTP access road.

17.6   **Left** on NTP going south.

19.9   Coles Creek (**W, RR**).

22.0   End of ride!

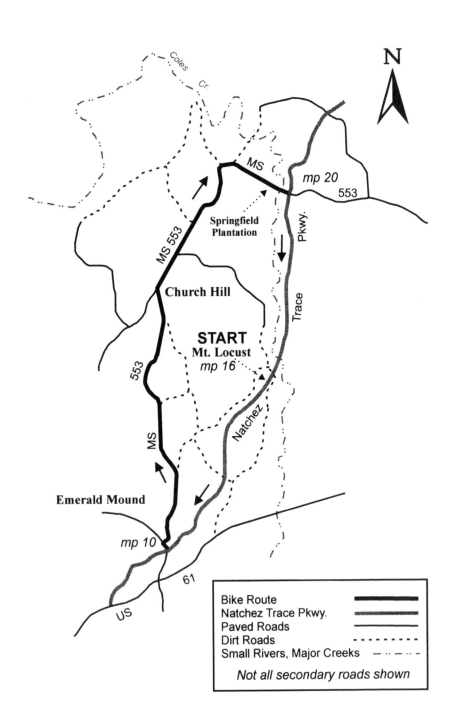

WINDSOR RUINS LOOP

Distance: 33 miles
Starting Point: Pullout at mp 29
Terrain: Moderately hilly.
Elev. Difference/Accumulated Climb: 200/1,000 ft.
Traffic: Light on all roads.
Combining Rides: *Church Hill Loop* (10 miles south on NTP), *Grand Gulf Loop, Vicksburg Tour.*

The Windsor Plantation home was reputed to be the grandest home in all of Mississippi. Judging by the some of the residences in Natchez, this claim may seem difficult to believe. But when you witness the 23 magnificent Corinthian columns standing today, you will probably agree that Windsor could have easily been the pinnacle of the plantation era. Built in 1859 by Smith Coffee Daniel II, it survived the Civil War unscathed, but later fell victim to a fire in 1890.

After a short initial stretch on the Natchez Trace, this trip heads west on MS 552 passing the Canemount Plantation en route to the Windsor Ruins. Canemount, an 1855 Italianate Revival home, is currently an elegant B&B featuring several cabins and hundreds of acres of forests and fields.

After leaving the Windsor Ruins, the terrain gets considerably hillier as Rodney Rd. heads up and down the Kudzu-filled ravines of the Loess Hills. On a high ridge over Bayou Pierre sits Point Lookout where a short dirt road leads to a replica of the first Presbyterian church in Mississippi and also offers views of Bayou Pierre.

Port Gibson makes an excellent refreshment stop in addition to providing a chance to stretch your legs by walking the shaded sidewalks along Church St. and viewing the historic homes. Ambitious cyclists can connect with the *Grand Gulf Loop* for a 77-mile trip.

Windsor Ruins

STARTING POINT: Park at the pullout at mp 29.3

Mile

0.0	Bike north on the NTP.
1.2	**Left** at the second exit for MS 552 at mp 30.5.
1.5	**Right** on MS 552 going north toward Alcorn. This will become Rodney Rd.
7.2	**Mkt, Rst**—Located .5 mi. to the left near the entrance to Alcorn University.
7.9	Canemount Plantation B&B (**Ldg**—see p. 60).
8.7	Bethel Church
11.3	Windsor Ruins. .3 mi. roundtrip on dirt road.
17.3	Pt. Lookout
21.5	Cross Main St. and continue on Carol St. in Port Gibson.
21.6	**Right** on Church St./US 61. **Mkt/Rst** to the left on Church St..
22.0	**Left** on Greenwood St. (becomes Magnolia St.).
22.5	**Right** on Bridewell Ln. (stop sign).
22.9	Cross MS 547 (stop sign).
24.5	**Left** on US 61 and immediately **right** on the NTP on-ramp (**Mkt**).
24.8	**Left** on the NTP going south.
33.0	End of ride!

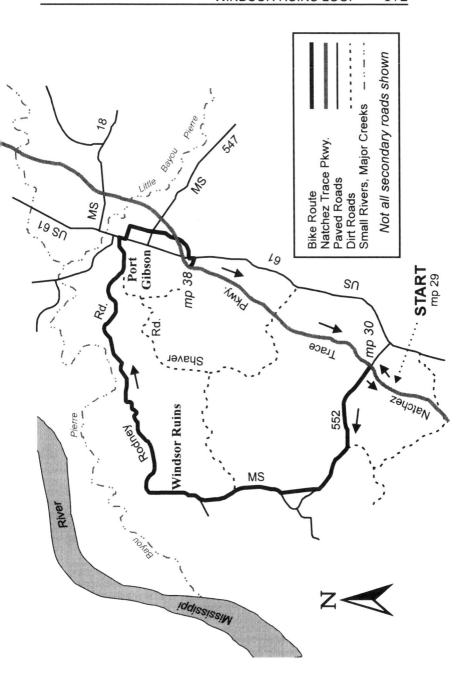

Bike Route
Natchez Trace Pkwy.
Paved Roads
Dirt Roads
Small Rivers, Major Creeks
Not all secondary roads shown

18

Bayou
Pierre

547

Little

MS

MS

US 61

61

US

Port
Gibson

mp 38

Pkwy.

START
mp 29

Rd.

Rd.

Trace

mp 30

Natchez

Shaver

552

Windsor Ruins

Pierre

Rodney

MS

River

Bayou

Mississippi

N

GRAND GULF LOOP

Distance: 45 miles
Starting Point: Rocky Springs (mp 55)
Terrain: Moderately hilly with a few short but very steep climbs.
Elev. Difference/Accumulated Climb: 270/1,160 ft.
Traffic: Light on all roads except near Pt. Gibson.
Combining Rides: *Windsor Ruins Loop, Vicksburg Tour.*

This ride has everything the Deep South is known for: sunken roads shaded by trees draped with Spanish moss, open fields of cotton, historic sites of vanished towns and Civil War battles, and a friendly town graced with lovely antebellum homes and churches. I rode this route on a sweltering August day and still managed to enjoy it even though the local people thought I was crazy.

After a pleasant 14-mile stretch on the Trace, this excursion heads into Port Gibson, the town that General Grant said was "too beautiful to burn." Here you will find markets, restaurants, and lodging (see p. 63). By continuing north on Church St./US 61 at mile 15.7, you can view several historic homes which have signs placed out front displaying the name and date of the house.

Leaving town, this route crosses Bayou Pierre. The first time I rode to Grand Gulf, the bridge was closed, but I was able to walk my bike across. The second time, I found the bridge was in the river! Fortunately when I was revising this book, I found a brand new bridge spanning the muddy bayou. After crossing Bayou Pierre, you will be treated to a pleasing stretch through the open pastures and fields that surround the Grand Gulf Nuclear Power Plant. In the unlikely event you should you hear a loud siren, simply follow the evacuation signs and RIDE AS FAST AS YOU CAN!

Grand Gulf State Historic Park is a fascinating place that very few people know about. In the 1830s, the town of Grand Gulf was a bustling port on the Mississippi River with 20 steamboats stopping every week. The town had several hotels, markets, and even a opera house. But the mighty river on which Grand Gulf prospered washed it away bit by bit. By 1860, 55 blocks had been eaten away by the changing course of the Mississippi River.

As if the river weren't enough, the Union gunboats bombarded the town in April of 1863. Unable to take Vicksburg, General Grant sent his forces down river to attempt to enter the state of Mississippi at Grand Gulf. But the guns of nearby Fort Cobun forced the Union fleet to withdraw here as well. Although the Confederates were initially successful at Vicksburg and Grand Gulf, the Union army entered Mississippi unopposed at Bruinsburg south of here.

Today the town is gone, but the state park features several reconstructions of historic buildings. A short loop road leads uphill to a lookout tower with a bird's eye view of the Mississippi River. You can also see the Confederate trenches used in defending Grand Gulf. The museum conveys the story of Grand Gulf plus features a variety of artifacts ranging from prehistoric Indians to Civil War times. Two short side trips lead to the site of Fort Cobun and the banks of the river.

After a long ride from Vicksburg, my German friend Roland and I arrived here just before dark as it began to rain. Luckily, we camped next to a picnic shelter with lights so our bikes and gear stayed dry while we had a relaxing dinner. The hot showers felt wonderful as well. To add to our fortunes, the rain stopped early the next morning!

A short but very steep hill heads out of Grand Gulf into the Loess Hills. This is my favorite section with narrow twisting roads sunken deep into the earth from years of wagon travel. The trees overhead shading the road were very welcomed on my August ride. This network of roads can be confusing, so follow the directions carefully. Eventually this route connects with Old Port Gibson Road which leads us back to the site of the vanished town Rocky Springs. When I rode this route, I continued to the Rocky Springs Church and then walked my bike down the 20-yard gravel path to the Parkway's parking area for this historic site. I later learned that the Park Service will not allow us to walk our bikes on any path (even for a few yards) so I rerouted this trip to connect with the Trace just south of here.

Sunken road near Grand Gulf

STARTING POINT: Rocky Springs (mp 54.8). Park at the restrooms, picnic area, or the Rocky Springs Historic Site. Do not park at the campground.

Mile

0.0	From the Rocky Springs entrance, bike south on the NTP. See p. 61 for historic sites and services.
13.6	Exit onto MS 18 (mp 41.3).
13.8	**Right** on MS 18 going west.
15.0	**Left** on Church St./US 61 (traffic light)(**Mkt**, **Rst**).
15.5	Cross Orange St. (traffic light)(**Supermkt**).
15.7	**Right** on Carol St. at the brick Baptist Church. (traffic light). Historic homes and churches are straight ahead within the next 5 blocks along Church St.
15.8	Cross Main St. (traffic light).
15.9	**Right** on Flower St. (first right after Main St.).
16.0	**Left** on Anthony St./Oil Mill Rd. (stop sign).
18.5	**Left** on Bald Hill Rd. after crossing Bayou Pierre.
23.7	**Left** on MS 18 (stop sign).
25.7	Grand Gulf State Park (**W**, **RR**, **PS**, **Cpg**). This is the last chance for water until Rocky Springs.
26.0	**Right** on unnamed road. (easy to miss).
26.1	**Left** on Back Grand Gulf Rd. and immediately start up a steep hill.
27.1	**Left**, staying on Back Grand Gulf Rd. , at the T-stop.
29.3	**Left** on Y-Camp Rd. (T-intersection).
30.9	**Right** on Karnack Ferry Rd. (YMCA Rd./Old Grand Gulf Rd.) (stop sign).
32.3	**Left** on Ingleside/Karnack Ferry Rd. at the T-intersection.
34.3	**Left** on US 61 (stop sign).
34.8	**Right** on Willow Rd. (first right).
37.7	**Left** on Old Port Gibson Rd. (stop sign at the 5-way intersection) which is the main road. Do not take the unnamed road that is a sharp left.
43.2	**Right** on Whiteaker Rd. (easy to miss—the NTP is barely visible from this intersection.)
43.3	**Left** on NTP going north.
45.2	End of ride!

Bike Route	▬▬▬▬▬
Natchez Trace Pkwy.	▬▬▬▬▬
Paved Roads	―――――
Dirt Roads	- - - - - -
Small Rivers, Major Creeks	— ·· — ·· —

Not all secondary roads shown

N

Mississippi River

Fisher Ferry Rd.

Natchez Trace Pkwy.

Black River

US 61

Big

Port Gibson Rd.

**Grand Gulf
Military Monument**

Rocky Springs

START
mp 55

Ingleside
Karnack Ferry
Rd.

Old

mp 53

Y-Camp
Rd.

Whiteaker Rd.

YMCA

Willow Rd.

Back
Gulf
Rd.

MS 462

Pierre

Grand Gulf Rd.

MS 18

Bayou

US 61

MS

Bald
Hill Rd.

Oil Mill Rd.

MS 18

Rodney Rd.

**Port
Gibson**

mp 41

MS 547

BRICES CROSS ROADS LOOP

Distance: 33 or 38 miles
Starting Point: Tupelo Visitor Center (mp 266)
Terrain: Mostly flat with a few hills.
Elev. Difference/Accumulated Climb: Option 1 -
100/340 ft.; Option 2 - 100/430 ft.
Traffic: Light to moderate on Birmingham Ridge Rd.
and MS 363. Light on all other roads.
Combining Rides: *Tupelo Tour*

The *Brices Cross Roads Loop* features peaceful roads meandering through a pleasant mix of rural farmland and scattered residential areas. When I stopped by Bicycle Pacelines, owner Brian Piazza mapped out numerous routes frequently ridden by Tupelo cyclists that also combine nicely with the Natchez Trace. This loop features two options that head out to Brices Cross Roads, a tiny National Battlefield in the middle of nowhere.

Things weren't at all peaceful on June 10, 1864 when the 3,500 Confederate soldiers led by General Nathan Bedford Forrest attacked the 8,100-man Union army of General Sturgis. The Union army, having been exhausted from marching on muddy roads and crossing swollen creeks, retreated toward Memphis. Forrest pressed the attack, and the orderly Union withdrawal became chaos. Artillery and wagons were abandoned, and 1,500 Union soldiers were captured in one of the last Confederate victories of the Civil War.

Leaving the battlefield, *Option 1* swings through the community of Saltillo, and *Option 2* runs through Guntown which, despite its name, is a sleepy little town. For those seeking a 49-mile trip, take MS 370 east from Brices Cross Roads. After going through the town of Baldwyn, this highway eventually connects with MS 371 just before the Natchez Trace.

One historical tidbit that Brian shared with me is the oldest paved road in the state is straight ahead where the *Brices Cross Roads Loop* turns left on Birmingham Ridge Rd. (at mile 2.4). This cement road crosses Mud Creek before connecting with Euclatubba Rd. on *Option 1*. Take a spin on it if you really want to experience some bumpy pavement!

Brices Cross Roads

STARTING POINT: Tupelo Visitor Center (mp 266.0)

Mile
0.0   From the visitor center, bike west on the access road directly opposite the mile post marker.

0.2   **Right** on CR 681 (stop sign at the T-intersection).

2.4   **Left** on Birmingham Ridge Rd. (stop sign).

10.8   Cross MS 348 and continue on CR 275 and 231 (stop sign)(**Mkt**).

16.0   **Right** on CR 883 (stop sign). MS 370 goes straight and to the left. Brices Cross Roads National Battlefield.
Go to Option 1 or Option 2

Option 1
33 miles
16.8   **Right** on CR 503 (first right).
19.1   Bear **left** on CR 2720.
19.8   **Right** on Euclatubba Rd./CR 601.
20.8   Cross MS 348 (stop sign).
23.8   **Left**, staying on Euclatubba Rd., where CR 251 goes right (stop sign).
25.5   Cross under US 45 and continue on 3rd St. (**Mkt**).
26.1   Cross MS 145 (stop sign) (**Mkt**).
27.0   **Rst**
27.4   **Left** on Mobile St./MS 363 (traffic light) in the town of Saltillo (**Mkt, Rst, Supermkt**).
28.7   **Right** on NTP access road.
28.8   **Right** on NTP going south. See p. 97 for historic sites and services.
33.4   End of ride!

Option 2
38 miles
21.3   **Left** on MS 348 (stop sign).
21.6   Cross over US 45.
21.8   **Mkt**
22.0   Cross MS 145 and continue on Main St. in the community of Guntown. (**Mkt**)
22.5   Straight onto Bryson St. where Main St. goes right. Bryson St. becomes CR 2578.
24.0   Bear **left** where CR 821 goes right.
26.3   **Right** on CR 1303/Friendship Rd. shortly after passing the Friendship Baptist Church.
27.4   **Right** on NTP access road.
27.5   **Right** on NTP going south. See p. 97 for historic sites and services.
37.5   End of ride!

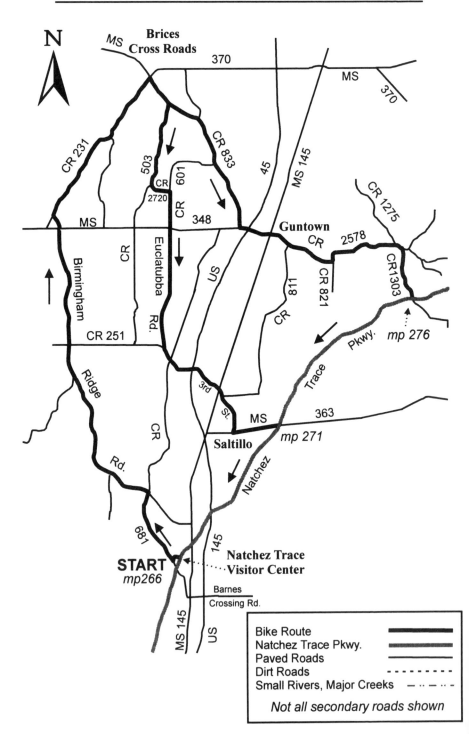

N

Brices
Cross Roads

MS
370

MS
370

CR 231

503

CR 833

CR
2720

CR 601

45

MS 145

CR 1275

MS

CR
348

Guntown

CR
2578

CR1303

Birmingham

CR

Euclatubba Rd.

US

CR 811

CR 821

CR 251

3rd

Trace

Pkwy.

mp 276

Ridge

CR

St.

MS
363

mp 271

Rd.

Saltillo

681

Natchez

145

START
mp266

Natchez Trace
Visitor Center

Barnes
Crossing Rd.

MS 145

US

Bike Route	▬▬▬▬
Natchez Trace Pkwy.	▬▬▬▬
Paved Roads	———
Dirt Roads	- - - -
Small Rivers, Major Creeks	—··—··—

Not all secondary roads shown

CHEROKEE LOOP

Distance: 16 miles
Starting Point: Colbert Ferry (mp 327)
Terrain: Flat to gentle rolling hills.
Elev. Difference/Accumulated Climb: 150/650 ft.
Traffic: Light except for 2 miles on the 4-lane US 72.
Combining Rides: The beginning of the *Florence Loop* is 2.6 miles north of Colbert Ferry.

This simple loop ride stretches between the sites of two stands operated by the half-Scot/Chickasaw brothers George and Levi Colbert. How a town named Cherokee came into existence on land formerly controlled by Chickasaw Indians is a mystery to me.

Regardless of the towns origins, the *Cherokee Loop* makes a pleasant excursion for those desiring a short and mostly flat day ride. For cyclists touring the Natchez Trace, this route through the little town of Cherokee adds only two miles and doesn't bypass any interpretive stops. With a popular country restaurant and a supermarket, this little dot on the map has helped numerous cyclists complete their journeys.

I particularly enjoyed pedaling the flat CR 21 following a bee line course through the cotton fields into Cherokee. Once in town, the food at the Wooden Nickel is definitely worth the stop, especially the home-made pies!

STARTING POINT: Colbert Ferry (mp 327.3)

Mile

0.0	Bike south on the NTP toward Tupelo.
1.1	**Left** on the CR 21 exit.
1.2	**Right** on CR 21/North Pike.
3.2	**Mkt**
5.9	**Right** on 2nd St. at the 4-way stop.
6.0	**Left** on Main St. (stop sign)(**Rst**).
6.1	**Right** on CR 20/Old Lee Highway after crossing RR tracks.
6.2	**Supermkt**
6.8	**Right** on US 72 (stop sign).
8.0	**Mkt**
8.5	**Left** on NTP access road.
9.3	**Left** on NTP going north.
16.4	End of ride!

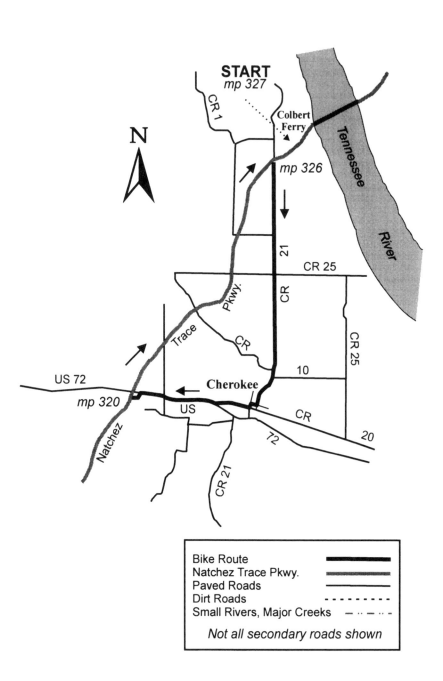

START
mp 327

CR 1

N

Colbert
Ferry

Tennessee

mp 326

CR 21

CR 25

Pkwy.

CR

River

CR

Trace

CR 25

US 72

10

Cherokee

mp 320

US

CR

72

20

Natchez

CR 21

Bike Route
Natchez Trace Pkwy.
Paved Roads
Dirt Roads ········
Small Rivers, Major Creeks — ·· — ·· —

Not all secondary roads shown

FLORENCE LOOP

Distance: 37 or 53 miles
Starting Point: Lauderdale Picnic Area (mp 329)
Terrain: Flat to moderately hilly.
Elev. Difference/Accumulated Climb: Option 1 - 250/920; Option 2 - 300/1,300 ft.
Traffic: Busy but tolerable near Florence. Light to moderate traffic on CR 14 and AL 157. Light on all other roads.
Combining Rides: *Cherokee Loop*—the start of this ride is 2.6 miles south of the Lauderdale Picnic area, *Tennessee River Tour.*

In the early days, this area was known for the treacherous shoals on the Tennessee River that caused more than a few boats to succumb to the river. Since then, the Florence/Muscle Shoals area has had more than a few claims to fame including residents such as **WC Handy**—the father of the blues, and **Helen Keller**.

The *Florence Loop* starts at the Tennessee River and heads through fields of cotton before reaching Florence. Just before the downtown area, a short detour leads to a unique home built by the renown architect **Frank Lloyd Wright**. This unimposing home built in 1940 with natural materials and a cantilever roof was Wright's dream to construct Usonian homes that the average American could afford.

The central business district of **Florence** has several interesting places to dine, plus numerous motels and B&Bs in the downtown area. Tours are given (admission) for the Wright home and the WC Handy Birthplace and Museum, both located in downtown. Call 888/FLO-TOUR for details.

Leaving town, our route passes the University of Northern Alabama after which *Option 1* and *Option 2* split with each route traveling through rural areas with frequent residences lining the roadway.

STARTING POINT: Lauderdale Picnic Area (mp 328.7)

Mile	
0.0	Bike north on NTP.
0.3	**Left** on the CR 2 exit.
0.5	**Left** on CR 2 going east toward Florence.
11.7	**Mkt**
15.3	**Right** on Coffee Rd./AL 20 (stop sign at the T-intersection).
16.4	**Left** on Beverly Ave. (easy to miss).
16.6	**Right** on Alabama St.
17.3	**Left** on Riverview Dr. Frank Lloyd Wright House is located to the right, then left to 601 Riverview Circle.
17.4	**Right** on Dr. Hicks Dr. (stop sign).
17.6	**Left** on Pine St. in downtown Florence (**Mkt, Rst, Ldg**). Restaurants located one block ahead on Court St. Call Tourism Bureau (256/740-4141) for dining and lodging info.
19.3	**Left** on Jackson Rd./CR 41 immediately after traffic light for Cypress Mill Rd. (**Mkt, Rst**).
20.6	Cross Cox Creek Pkwy.
23.3	Continue straight where CR 16 enters from the right.

Go to Option 1 or Option 2

Option 1

37 miles

23.7	**Left** on CR 16 and begin downhill to creek.
25.3	Cross CR 200 (stop sign).
25.7	Cross AL 20 (stop sign) (**Mkt**).
27.5	Cross CR 15 (stop sign).
28.8	**Left** on CR 81 and immediately **right** on CR 14 (confusing intersection)(**Mkt**).
33.7	**Right** on NTP access road.
33.9	**Right** on NTP going south.
37.2	End of ride!

Option 2
53 miles

23.7   Continue straight on CR 121/41 where CR 16 goes left.

25.6   **Right** on CR 9 (stop sign at the T-intersection).

25.9   **Left** on AL 157 (stop sign at the T-intersection).

30.2   **Mkt, Rst**

32.1   **Mkt**

34.8   Optional shortcut to Parkway by going left on CR 10.

35.9   Bear **left** on Cypress Creek Rd. after crossing the TN line.

36.3   **Mkt**

38.0   **Left** on NTP going south. See p.105 for historic sites and services.

53.0   End of ride!

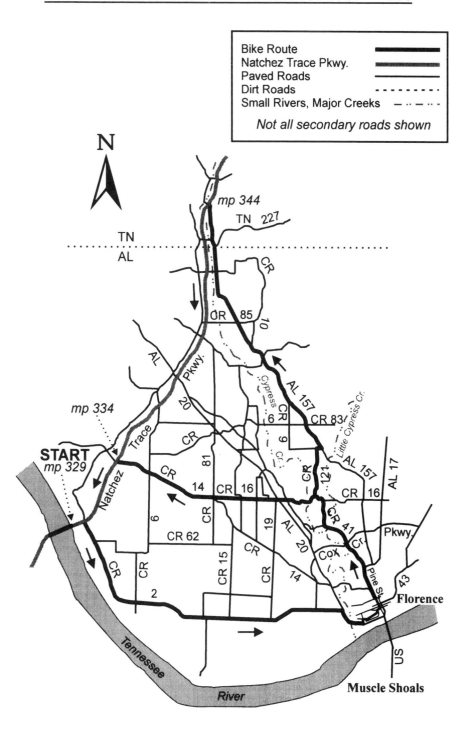

BUFFALO VALLEY LOOP

Distance: 20, 53, or 77 miles
Starting Point: Meriwether Lewis Historic Site (mp 386)
Terrain: Flat to hilly on all options. Several challenging climbs on all options.
Elev. Difference/Accumulated Climb: Option 1 - 350/900 ft.; Option 2 - 350/2,400 ft.; Option 3 - 400/2,920 ft.
Traffic: Moderate on TN 20 and TN 13. Heavy traffic on wide-shouldered US 64. Light on all other roads.
Combining Rides: *Tennessee River Tour, Snow Creek Tour.*

Although the buffalo are gone, the Buffalo River continues to flow as the last untamed river in Middle Tennessee. And this ride is worthy of the river it follows. Fortunately, you have the first 6 miles to warm up on a lovely stretch along Grinders Creek because the climbing begins just before reaching TN 99. The first big climb is followed by a fun drop to the Buffalo River. Upon leaving TN 99, *Option 1* immediately delivers another very steep climb followed by a descent to Chief Creek and Napier Lake.

On *Option 2* and *Option 3*, it's one hill after another with some being quite long. Superb scenery, good pavement, and light traffic make this ride worth the effort. To truly experience this area, consider doing your own biathlon by adding a half-day canoe trip on the Buffalo River. This route goes by Buffalo River Canoeing and Campground (800/339-5596 or 931/796-5596) on TN 99.

The town square in Waynesboro makes an excellent lunch stop for *Option 3* and is a 7-mile roundtrip detour on *Option 2*. Here you can enjoy a country cookin' lunch and browse in the various shops.

Option 2 heads east to the Trace on US 64, a busy highway with wide paved shoulders. *Option 3* follows TN 13, then hooks up with a delightful country road along the Green River before rejoining TN 13 after a short but grueling climb.

STARTING POINT: Meriwether Lewis Historic Site (mp 385.9). Park by the log cabin/museum which is .5 mi. off the Parkway.

Mile

0.0   Bike toward TN 20 and the NTP.

0.3   **Right** on TN 20 going west toward Hohenwald (stop sign at the T-intersection).

2.0   **Left** on Grinders Cr. Rd.

6.5   **Left**, staying on Grinders Cr. Rd. where Rush Br. Rd. goes straight.

7.5   **Left** on TN 99 West (really south) (stop sign). *Go to Option 1, Option 2, or Option 3*

Option 1
20 miles

9.2   **Left** on Napier Rd. (Napier Lake Rd.) immediately after crossing the Buffalo River.

14.5   **Right** on NTP access road (**Mkt**—.5 mi. straight ahead).

14.6   **Left** on NTP toward Nashville.

19.7   **Left** at Meriwether Lewis Site/TN 20 exit.

20.1   End of ride!

Option 2
53 miles

14.3   **Left**, staying on TN 99, at stop sign.

14.9   **Right**, staying on TN 99.

28.9   **Left** on Old Hwy. 64 where TN 99 goes right (stop sign at the T-intersection). Services (**Mkt, Rst, Ldg**) available in Waynesboro. Follow *Option 3* for 3-4 mi. from this intersection.

30.0   **Left** on US 64 (stop sign at the T-intersection).

36.1	**Mkt**, **Ldg**.
36.7	**Right** on NTP access road after going under the parkway.
36.9	**Right** on NTP. See p. 105 for historic sites and services.
52.9	**Left** at Meriwether Lewis Site/TN 20 exit.
53.3	End of ride!

Option 3
77 miles

14.3	**Left**, staying on TN 99, at stop sign.
14.9	**Right**, staying on TN 99.
28.9	**Right**, staying on TN 99, at the stop sign. **Supermkt**, **Ldg**, and **Rst** are within the next 4 mi. See p. 153 for lodging info.
31.6	**Right** on US 64 (traffic light).
32.3	Straight onto Dexter Woods Memorial Blvd. at the taffic light.
32.9	Do a 3/4 circle around the courthouse in Waynesboro and go **right** on TN 13 South (also Main St.).
35.0	**Left** on Upper Green River Rd. (Green River Access) by the red-brick Green River Baptist Church.
38.2	Bear **right** and begin uphill.
40.0	Bear **left** and immediately turn **left** again on TN 13 (stop sign at the T-intersection).
42.3	**Mkt**, **Rst**.
44.6	**Left** on Broadway in Collinwood (stop sign). **Mkt**, **Rst**, and **Supermkt** to the right on TN 13.
44.7	**Left** on NTP access road.
44.8	**Left** on NTP toward Nashville. See p. 105 for historic sites and services.
76.4	**Left** at Meriwether Lewis Site/TN 20 exit.
76.8	End of ride!

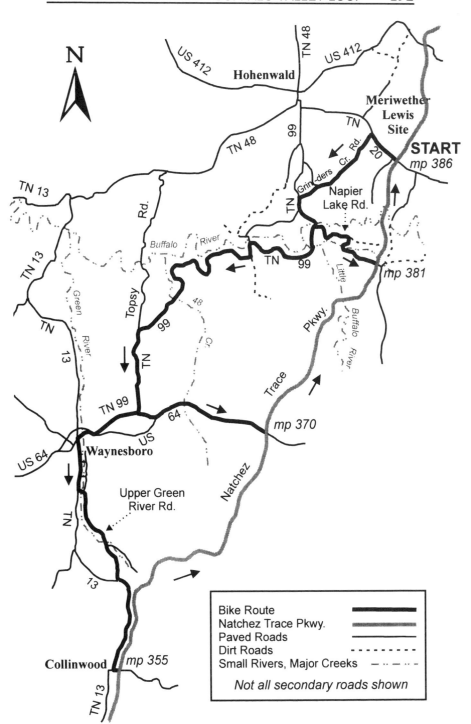

N

US 412
TN 48
US 412
Hohenwald

Meriwether Lewis Site

TN 48
99
TN
Grinders Cr. Rd.
20
START
mp 386

Napier Lake Rd.

TN 13

Rd.

Buffalo *River*
TN 99
TN 13
Little
mp 381

Green
River
Topsy
48 Cr.
99
TN
Buffalo River
Pkwy.
Trace

TN 13

TN 99
64
mp 370

US 64
Waynesboro
US

Natchez

Upper Green River Rd.

TN

13

Collinwood *mp 355*

TN 13

Bike Route	▬▬▬
Natchez Trace Pkwy.	▬▬▬
Paved Roads	——
Dirt Roads	- - - -
Small Rivers, Major Creeks	—·—·—

Not all secondary roads shown

LEIPERS CREEK LOOP

Distance: 29, 40, or 48 miles
Starting Point: Garrison Branch (mp 428)
Terrain: Moderately hilly. Most grades are gradual except for two short steep climbs on *Option 2.*
Elev. Difference/Accumulated Climb: Option 1 - 380/1,050 ft.; Option 2 - 440/1,780 ft.; Option 3 - 490/2,210 ft.
Traffic: Light to moderate on TN 50, Old Hillsboro Rd., and TN 7. Light on all other roads.
Combining Rides: *Fernvale Loop, Option 3 of Backbone Ridge Loop.*

This is truly a gem of a ride. It is easy to see why these options have long been favorites of the Nashville Bicycle Club and other cyclists who have discovered how to combine a variety of idyllic rural roads with the Natchez Trace Parkway.

The first portion of this ride heads up a gentle grade along Leipers Fork before reaching the top of the Tennessee Valley Divide. On the other side, the road descends along Leipers Creek, an entirely different stream that flows into the Duck River rather than the Harpeth River. This side of the watershed was Indian territory during the days that the boatmen traveled the Trace. *Option 1* continues along this creek to the town of Fly with a garage, lumber mill, and classic country market.

Option 2 and *Option 3* follow Sulphur Creek back up to the ridge where our route rolls through the town of Theta. Shortly after Theta, a hair-raising descent takes you off the ridge and into the beautiful Snow Creek Valley. Cyclists can easily exceed 40 mph here, but there is a dangerous sharp left at the bottom. Brake well before you get to this turn or you will meet a barbed wire fence!

Option 2 and *Option 3* split in the town of Santa Fe (pronounced Santa Fee) where you can replenish your spent calories at the two markets or the country restaurant. *Option 2* embarks on a roller coaster route through the peaceful Water Valley while *Option 3* follows Snow Creek to the Natchez Trace Parkway at the Duck River.

Jackson Falls at mp 404.7 (3 miles south of where Option 3 joins the Trace)

STARTING POINT: Garrison Branch (mp 427.6)

Mile
0.0   Bike north (toward Nashville) on the NTP.
1.5   **Left** on the TN 46/Pinewood Rd. exit.
1.8   **Right** on TN 46/Pinewood Rd. going east.
2.4   **Right** on Leipers Creek Rd. (Old Hillsboro Rd.)
           (stop sign at the T-intersection).
5.9   **Mkt**
           Go to Option 1 or Options "2 & 3"

Option 1
29 miles

12.2   **Mkt**
15.1   **Right** on TN 7 (stop sign at the T-intersection) (**Mkt**).
17.0   **Right** on the access road to the NTP immediately after going under the Parkway bridge.
17.2   **Left** on the NTP (going north). See p. 112 for historic sites and services.
28.8   End of ride!

Options "2 & 3"
40 or 48 miles

9.3   **Left** on Sulphur Springs Branch Rd. (first left after a substantial descent).
12.2   **Right** on Snow Creek Rd./TN 247 (Dodson Rd.) (stop sign at the T-intersection) (**Mkt**).
    Go to Option 2 or Option 3

Option 2

18.7   **Right** on TN 7 in the town of Santa Fe (stop sign at the 4-way intersection). (**Mkt, Rst**).
19.4   Go straight onto Water Valley Rd. where TN 7 turns sharply to the right.
23.3   **Right** on Leipers Creek Rd. in the community of Water Valley. (**Ldg**) Water Valley B&B $$$ (931/682-2266).
26.8   **Left** on TN 7 (stop sign at the T-intersection).
28.0   **Right** on the access road to the NTP immediately after going under the Parkway bridge.
28.2   **Left** on the NTP (going north). See p. 113 for historic sites and services.
39.9   End of ride!

Option 3

18.7   Cross TN 7 at Santa Fe (**Mkt, Rst**).
25.0   **Right** on TN 50 (stop sign at the T-intersection).
28.0   **Right** onto the NTP access road and go north toward Nashville. (**W, RR, PS, Mkt, Cpg**) Gordon Ferry historic site is .4 mi. to the south on the Parkway. See p. 112 for historic sites and services.
47.5   End of ride!

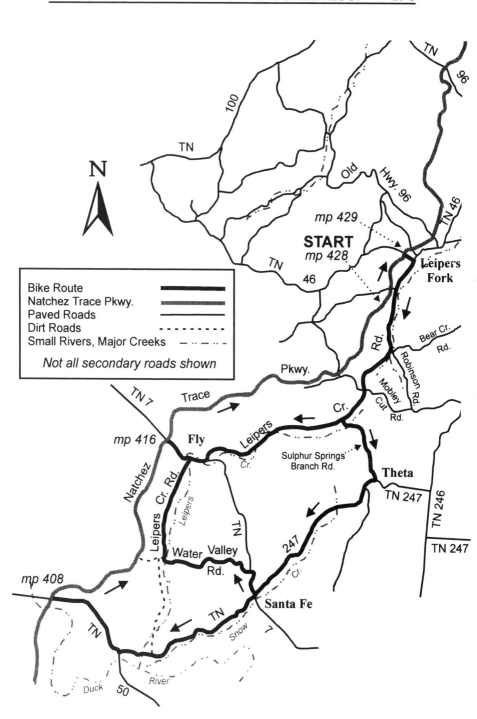

N

Bike Route
Natchez Trace Pkwy.
Paved Roads
Dirt Roads
Small Rivers, Major Creeks

Not all secondary roads shown

TN 96

TN 100

TN

Old Hwy. 96

mp 429

START
mp 428

TN 46

Leipers
Fork

TN 46

Bear Cr. Rd.

Rd.

Robinson Rd.

Mobley Cut Rd.

Pkwy.

Trace

Leipers Cr.

TN 7

mp 416

Fly

Cr.

Sulphur Springs
Branch Rd.

Theta

TN 247

TN 246

Natchez

Leipers Cr. Rd.

Leipers

TN

Water Valley Rd.

247

Cr.

TN 247

mp 408

TN

TN 7

Santa Fe

Snow

Duck River

50

FERNVALE LOOP

Distance: 28 or 35 miles
Starting Point: TN 96 Bridge (mp 438)
Terrain: Hilly with a few challenging climbs. Several flat to rolling sections.
Elev. Difference/Accumulated Climb: Option 1 - 400/1,160 ft.; Option 2 - 400/1,150 ft.
Traffic: TN 96 has wide paved shoulders and heavy traffic. Light to moderate on Pinewood Rd. Light on all other roads.
Combining Rides: *Backbone Ridge Loop, Leipers Creek Loop.*

The rural roads of the *Fernvale Loop* have been popular with local cyclists long before the Natchez Trace Parkway was completed. After pedaling among horse farms, hardwood forests, and cascading creeks, I think you'll see why. In the early 1900s, the community of Fernvale was known for one of the largest mineral spring resorts in the area. Today, it is known to many as home of one of the toughest hills in the area. You too can experience this challenging climb (nearly 300 feet in half a mile) just two miles beyond Fernvale on *Option 1.* Try admiring the densely wooded hillside rather than thinking about the climb up Backbone Ridge.

The peaceful town of Leipers Fork with two markets, a country restaurant, and a B&B is accustomed to having cyclists rolling through the area. (See p. 113 for accommodations.) The *Leipers Creek Loop* begins just south of here and combines nicely with the *Fernvale Loop* for extended day rides. In addition to the Natchez Trace, there are miles of excellent cycling roads in the area. You could do a different ride each day for an entire week! Our book **Bicycling Middle Tennessee** includes several additional day rides.

STARTING POINT: TN 96 Bridge Overlook (mp 438.2)

0.0   Bike south on the NTP going away from Nashville.
0.8   **Left** on the TN 96 exit at mp 437.4.
1.4   **Left** on TN 96 going west (stop sign at the T-intersection).
4.0   **Left** on Old Harding Rd. just before crossing the South Harpeth River.
       Go to Option 1 or Option 2

Option 1
28 miles

8.9   Continue straight on Old Hwy. 96 (3-way stop) in the community of Fernvale.
14.3   **Right** on Hargrove Rd. (first right after climbing Backbone Ridge).
14.7   **Left** on Wilkins Branch Rd. (Wilkie Branch Rd.)(first left).
17.4   **Right** on Old Hillsboro Rd./TN 46 (stop sign) (**Mkt**).
17.6   **Right** on Pinewood Rd./TN 46 (first right).
18.2   **Left** on NTP access road.
18.5   **Left** on NTP going north toward Nashville.
27.7   End of ride!

Option 2
35 miles

8.9   **Right** on Old Hwy. 96 (3-way stop) in the community of Fernvale.
9.0   **Left** on Caney Fork Rd. (first left).
14.5   **Left** on Deer Ridge Rd. (stop sign at the T-intersection).
16.0   **Left** on Pinewood Rd./TN 46 (stop sign at the T-intersection).
18.4   **Mkt**
25.7   **Right** on NTP access road (**Mkt**—.6 mi. ahead on TN 46).
26.0   **Left** on NTP going north.
35.2   End of ride!

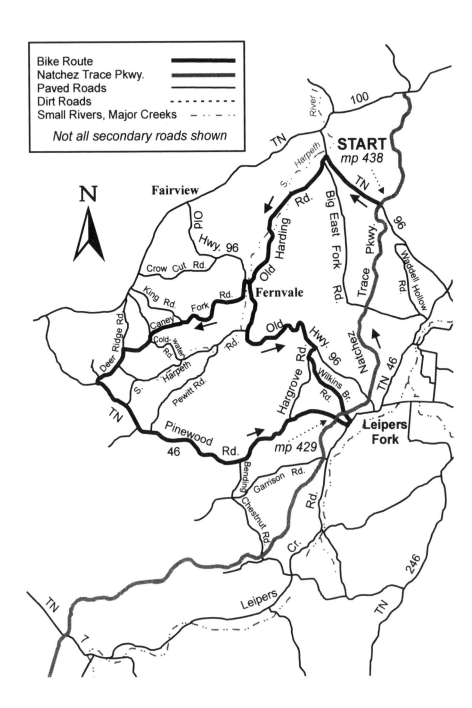

BACKBONE RIDGE LOOP

Distance: 17, 23, or 35 miles
Starting Point: Northern Terminus (mp 442)
Terrain: 3 challenging climbs with flat to rolling terrain
in between.
Elev. Difference/Accumulated Climb: Option 1 -
400/850 ft.; Option 2 - 400/850 ft.; Option 3 -
400/1,080 ft.
Traffic: Heavy traffic on the wide shouldered TN 96.
Moderate to heavy for a short distance near Frank-
lin. Light to moderate on TN 46 and Southall Rd.
on *Option 3*. Light on all other roads.
Combining Rides: *Fernvale Loop, Leipers Creek
Loop* (*Option 3* only).

Nashville cyclists are fortunate to have a wealth of excellent road riding only 15 miles from downtown. From the Northern Terminus, many fine loop possibilities exist as long as you avoid busy TN 100.

While most Nashvillians don't even know Backbone Ridge exists, local cyclists certainly do! This 200+ foot ridge divides the South Harpeth and Harpeth Rivers. *Option 1* and *Option 2* will give you the pleasure of climbing Backbone Ridge three times while *Option 3* conquers it twice. But don't chicken out, the scenery is definitely worth the effort.

Option 2 and *Option 3* swing within four miles of the historic town of Franklin, a cyclists' heaven complete with bakery, ice cream shop, restaurants, and, yes, even a Star-bucks! All options return via Old Natchez Trace (part of the original Trace), a narrow shaded lane that follows the Har-peth River and passes antebellum homes, Indian mounds, and the stone pilings of a bridge built in 1801.

This ride connects nicely with the *Fernvale Loop* and *Option 3* joins the *Leipers Creek Loop*. As you can see, there is no shortage of excellent riding in this area.

Remains of original Natchez Trace bridge along Old Natchez Trace

STARTING POINT: Northern Terminus (mp 442.2). Park along TN 100. To postpone the initial "big" climb until the end of the ride, you may park at the site of the future Visitor Center 2 miles down the Parkway.

Begin with Option 1, Option 2, or Option 3

Option 1
17 miles

Mile

0.0	Bike south on NTP. (Begin milage at mp 442.0)
4.6	**Left** on the TN 96 exit at mp 437.4.
5.2	**Right** on TN 96 at the bottom of the access road.
8.7	**Left** on TN 46/Old Hillsboro Rd. (flashing yellow light).
11.0	**Left** on Old Natchez Trace (easy to miss).
12.5	**Left** on Temple Rd.

14.9   **Left** on Sneed Rd. (Union Bridge Rd.)(stop sign) which becomes Pasquo Rd.

16.1   **Left** on TN 100 (stop sign at the T-intersection).

16.6   End of ride!

Option 2
23 miles

0.0   Bike south on the NTP. (Begin milage at mp 442.0)

4.6   **Left** on the TN 96 exit at mp 437.4.

5.2   **Right** on TN 96 at the bottom of the access road.
       Go to Options "2 & 3"

Option 3
35 miles

0.0   Bike south on the NTP. (Begin milage at mp 442.0)

13.0   **Right** on the TN 46/Pinewood Rd. exit at mp 429.0. This is the second exit for TN 46.

13.3   **Right** on TN 46 going east.

13.9   **Left** on TN 46/Old Hillsboro Rd. (stop sign at the T-intersection)(**Mkt**).

15.2   Town of Leipers Fork (**Mkt, Rst, Ldg**).

15.7   **Right** on Southall Rd. (Old Hwy. 96).

17.3   **Left** on McMillan Rd. (first left).

17.9   **Left** on Boxley Valley Rd. (first left).

19.3   **Left** on Blazer Rd. (stop sign at the T-intersection).

19.7   **Right** on Boyd Mill Rd. (stop sign at the T-intersection).

22.4   **Right** on TN 96 (stop sign).
       Go to Options "2 & 3"

Options "2 & 3"

10.6, 22.6   **Left** on Short Rd. (Old Charlotte Pk.). Downtown Franklin is 3 mi. ahead on TN 96. To rejoin route from Franklin, bike north on US 431/5th Ave., then go left on Del Rio Pk.

12.1, 24.1   Straight onto Carlisle Ln. at the stop sign.

12.3, 24.3   Straight onto Del Rio Pk. (3-way stop).

13.9, 15.9	**Left** (staying on Del Rio Pk.) at the next 3-way stop.
15.8, 27.8	**Right** on Old Hillsboro Rd./TN 46 (stop sign at the T-intersection).
15.9, 27.9	**Left** on Old Natchez Trace (first left).
18.4, 30.4	**Left** on Temple Rd.
20.8, 32.8	**Left** on Sneed Rd. (Union Bridge Rd.)(stop sign) which becomes Pasquo Rd.
22.0, 34.0	**Left** on TN 100 (stop sign at the T-intersection).
22.5, 34.5	End of ride!

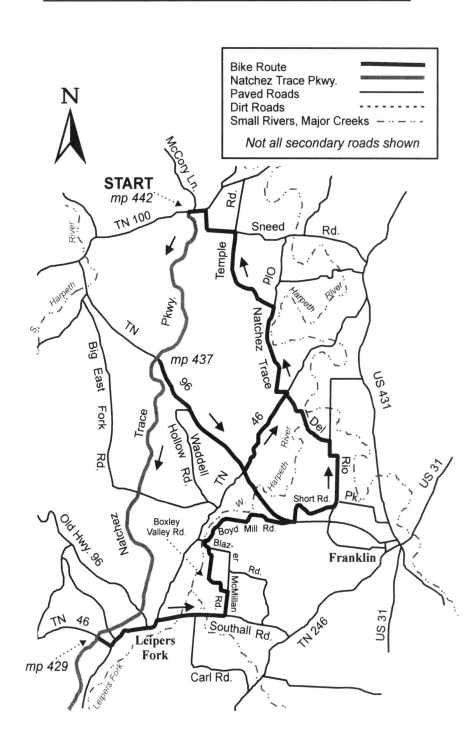

PERCY WARNER PARK LOOP

Distance: 2-11 miles
Starting Point: Belle Meade Entrance to Percy Warner Park in Nashille
Terrain: Constantly hilly. A thrilling and challenging roller coaster-type route.
Elev. Difference/Accumulated Climb: 360/1,100 ft.
Traffic: Light.
Combining Rides: Half of the one way loop can replace a portion of the bike route between Nashville and the Parkway.

The *Percy Warner Park Loop* is a wonderful 11-mile ride among lush forests and meadows on a narrow winding one-way road with very little motorized traffic. Although none of the Parkway is utilized, the original Trace did run through this area. This ride is, in my opinion, one of the best short road rides anywhere.

The 11-mile Main Drive is not well marked so follow these directions very carefully. The road system is basically one big loop with five cutoffs or shortcuts that return to the Main Drive, thus creating shorter loops ranging from 2 to 10 miles. You can easily extend this trip by crossing Old Hickory Blvd. (caution—blind hill with fast traffic) and continuing on the closed road system (no motor vehicles) in Edwin Warner Park.

The Warner Parks combine to form one of the largest city parks in the country, providing a 2,700-acre nature sanctuary for a large variety of trees, plants, and wildlife. From the Main Drive, a short .6-mile loop goes up to Lea's Summit (elevation 920 ft.) offering a wonderful view of the Nashville Basin and the downtown skyline.

The route is very hilly with several steep climbs rising 200 feet in half a mile. On the descents, be very careful when navigating the many sharp blind curves, watching out especially for two nasty hairpin turns near the end of the loop.

STARTING POINT: Belle Meade Entrance. From Nashville, take West End Ave./Harding Rd./US 70S away from Nashville and turn left on Belle Meade Blvd. Continue until it ends at the park entrance.

Mile

0.0   Bike into the park on the one-way Main Drive.

0.7   Bear **right** at the first junction. (Cut-off #1 goes left.)

1.8   Stay **left** at the next intersection. Don't take the road to TN 100.

2.1   Deep Well Picnic Area and Trailhead. Continue straight.

3.3   Continue straight after the long climb. (Cut-off #2 goes left.)

3.9   Stay **right** at the "Y" before the picnic shelter. (Cut-off #3 goes left.)

4.2   Continue straight. (Cut-off #4 goes left.)

4.8   Make a hard **left** (4-way intersection) immediately past the two picnic shelters. Several one-way roads with DO NOT ENTER signs will join the Main Drive.

5.1   .4-mi. two-way road to right connects with Vaughn Rd. This is on the bike route between the Natchez Trace and Nashville.

6.5   Golf course and clubhouse on the right. (Begin two-way traffic.)

7.1   Continue straight at the 4-way intersection. (Cut-off #5 goes left. Begin one-way traffic.)

8.5   Veer **right** at Beech Woods Picnic area. (Cut-off #5 will enter from the left.)

9.1   Turn **right** where a one-way road (Cut-off #2) enters from the left.

10.2   Road to Lea's Summit goes to the left, loops around, and comes back (.6-mi. roundtrip).

10.7   Turn **right** where a one-way street (Cut-off #1) enters from the left.

11.2   End of ride! Back into civilization!

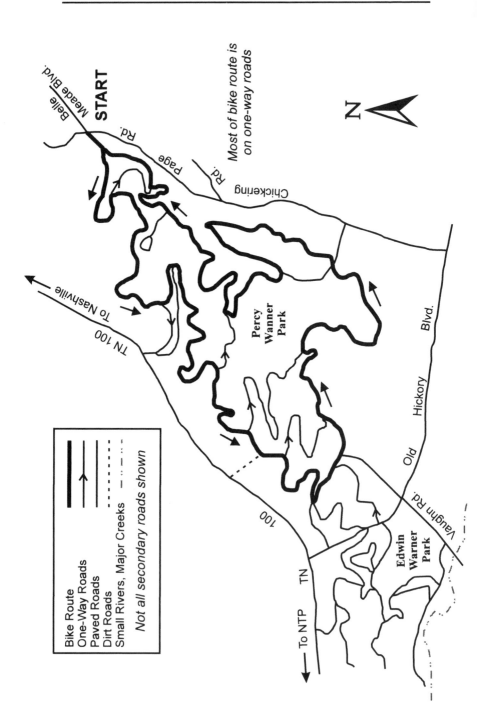

START

Belle Meade Blvd.

Most of bike route is on one-way roads

N

Page Rd.

Chickering Rd.

To Nashville

TN 100

Percy Warner Park

Hickory Blvd.

Old

Vaughn Rd.

Edwin Warner Park

100

TN

To NTP

Bike Route

One-Way Roads

Paved Roads

Dirt Roads

Small Rivers, Major Creeks

Not all secondary roads shown

ADDITIONAL DAY RIDES

If the eleven day rides included in this book are not enough for you, here are some other possibilities:

South of Jackson (mp 53-87) I am told that the better cycling near Jackson is to the south. Parking possibilities include the town of Clinton (on the *Jackson Bypass*), the Battle of Raymond interpretive stop (mp 78.3), or Rocky Springs (mp 54.8). From Clinton, you can bike south to Raymond (moderately busy) and then take MS 467 back to the Parkway, or continue south on Port Gibson Street and Old Port Gibson Road. From Old Port Gibson Road, you can connect with the Trace via MS 27 (mp 66.5), Fisher Ferry Road (mp 59.1), or Whitaker Road (mp 52.8).

Another possibility is to follow the *Vicksburg Tour* to Edwards and then take Mt. Moriah Road or Smith Station Road, both which connect to Middle Road which in turn intersects with Old Port Gibson Road. The maps on p. 144 and p. 177 show the route possibilites better than I can explain them. The only roads to avoid (except for necessary short stretches) are MS 27 and MS 18, both of which have fast truck traffic.

Tupelo (mp 260-266) For a pleasant urban excursion, bike the *Tupelo Tour* (p. 87) and return on the Trace for a 24 mile loop.

Waterloo (mp 330-353) A wonderful 80-mile loop can be created by combining *Option 1* and *Option 2* of *Day 3* of the *Tennessee River Tour*. Park at Rock Springs (mp 330.2) or McGlamery Stand (mp 352.9). You can cut off 4 miles by bypassing Colinwood which entails walking around a gate between TN 13 and the Trace at McGlamery Stand (see p. 155 for instructions). Weatherford Creek Road also provides a more substantial short cut. See map on p. 159.

Swan Creek (mp 386-408) An ideal figure eight loop may be ridden by combining the Natchez Trace with idyllic roads through the Swan Valley. Park at Meriwether Lewis (mp 385.9), Phosphate Mine (mp 390.7), or Gordon Ferry (mp 407.7). The 21-mile southern loop follows the spur to The Farm that is listed in the *Snow Creek Tour.* When you get to TN 20, go right (west) toward the Trace. The 44-mile northern loop uses *Option 2* on *Day 2* of the same tour. Both loops can be combined for a challenging 65-mile ride. If this isn't enough, add *Option 1* of the *Buffalo Valley Loop,* and you have a honest century with tough hills thrown in for no extra charge! See the map on p. 166.

The author enjoys a trip down the Trace with his family

OUTDOOR RECREATION

Besides road cycling, the Natchez Trace region offers an abundance of activities for the outdoor enthusiast. While many of nature trails only require a few minutes, other activities like canoeing can keep you entertained all day.

Hiking

Numerous nature trails are found all along the Parkway. The following is a list of hikes over one mile in length.

Coles Creek (mp 17) A 3.5-mile trail follows the Old Trace through subtropical forest.

Rocky Springs (mp 55) Up to 10 miles of trail including a trail to the Owens Creek waterfall. Portions of the Old Trace are used.

Jeff Busby (mp 193) A 1-mile trail leads to the top of Little Mountain.

Witch Dance (mp 233) Over 10 miles of horse trails in the Tombigbee National Forest. These trails are often very muddy after heavy rains.

Parkway Headquarters and Visitor Center (mp 266) A 4.5-mile trail leads to the Old Town Overlook and continues to Chickasaw Village.

Tishomingo State Park (mp 303) Over 10 miles of trail meander through this unique rocky landscape shaded by mature pine and hardwood forests. Features a suspension bridge over Bear Creek. In my opinion, this is some of the best hiking along the Parkway.

Meriwether Lewis Site (mp 386) Over 5 miles of trail follow the Old Trace and the course of the pristine Little Swan Creek.

Devil's Backbone State Natural Area (mp 394) Several miles of hiking trails meander from ridges to remote hollows.

Garrison Creek (mp 428) A 25-mile horse and hiking trail follows the ridge to the Tennessee Valley Divide and continues south to TN 7.

Mountain Biking

Although mountain bikes are prohibited on all trails on Parkway property, there are a few opportunities to leave the pavement from the Trace. Many more possibilities are a short drive by car. Remember, it is your responsibility to know the current regulations, and please don't ride on any trail if doing so will cause further damage. Like elsewhere in the country, trail access is often controversial in the Southeast, so proper etiquette is essential. Control your speed and always yield to other users.

Clear Springs Recreation Area/Homochitto National Forest (Natchez) The hot spot for mountain biking in southern Mississippi is a half hour drive east of Natchez on US 84. Features 17 miles of jeep road and single track.

Mt. Locust (mp 16) A series of graded dirt roads parallel the Parkway to the west. The deep sunken roads are very scenic and ideal for casual mountain or hybrid cyclists. From Mt. Locust, bike south on the Parkway and go right on the dirt road at mp 13. In 1.4 miles, go right again. Stay to the right on all open (non-gated) roads and in a little more than 3 miles, you will return to the Parkway just north of Mt. Locust.

Forest Hill Park (mp 87) 25 miles away via interstate, this city park in Jackson features 5 miles of double and singletrack. Take I-20 east, I-55 south, and then go west on Savannah St.

Witch Dance (mp 233) Over 10 miles of horse trails in the Tombigbee National Forest are currently open to bikes. Expect a few steep hills. These trails are often very muddy and are not recommended after heavy rains.

Trace State Park (mp 260) Located 9 miles west on MS 6, this state park features several miles of challenging trails also used by ATV's.

Tombigbee Waterway (mp 293) A flat gravel access road runs along the west side of the waterway. From the south side of the Parkway bridge, carefully walk your bike down the grass embankment. Wetlands provide excellent bird watching opportunities.

Wildwood Park (mp 332) Located 15 miles east of the Parkway on AL 14, this nature park on the outskirts of Florence offers 10 miles of excellent single track with intermediate hills. If you are coming from the Trace, the parking area is to the right just after crossing Cypress Creek. The trail begins near the bridge on the north side of AL 14.

Laurel Hill Wildlife Management Area (mp 376) Start on the Old Trace Drive and go right at the next junction, then keep left where another road goes under the Parkway. This graded dirt road takes you down to the Little Buffalo River. A few faint jeep tracks are available for exploring. By going left on the second graded road after crossing the Little Buffalo, it is possible to connect with the Old Trace Drive. Many miles of dirt roads are open to mountain bikers but I suggest you avoid hunting season during the fall.

Chickasaw County Park (mp 416) Seven miles of single track trails built by the Columbia Bike Club are approximately 13 miles east toward the Columbia.

Bowie Nature Park (mp 437) Located 12 miles away in the town of Fairview (go west on TN 96, then left on TN 100), this nature park features 10 miles of jeep roads and single track complete with moderate hills and slick stream crossings.

Hamilton Creek Recreation Area (Northern Terminus) Located 25 miles away along Percy Priest Lake on the east side of Nashville, the metro park contains an intermediate and advance loop—all single track. The advance loop is extremely technical with numerous rock ledges, steep climbs, and difficult maneuvering. From I-40, take Stewarts Ferry Pk./Bell Rd. south.

Canoeing

Bear Creek (mp 303) Tishomingo State Park (662/438-6914) offers an 8-mile Class I (easy) float trip. Dismals Canyon Campground (800/808-7998) and Canoe Rental, located 30 miles off the Trace, can sometimes arrange to pick up cyclists to run some of Alabama's best whitewater along a rugged portion of upper Bear Creek.

Buffalo River (mp 383) With nearly 100 free-flowing miles, the Buffalo is the premier canoeing river in Middle Tennessee. Clear rippling shoals, limestone bluffs, and hardwood forests make this an unforgettable trip. The put-in at Metal Ford is recommended only in relatively high water. Jim Hobbs, owner of Buffalo River Canoeing (800/339-5596 or 931/796-5596) will pick up cyclists from the Trace. He will even take your bikes while you float to his campground along the river 13 miles from the Trace. Riverside Canoeing and Camping (931/796-2326) offers the same services and is located 8 miles from the Trace. Crazy Horse Park (800/722-5213 or 931/722-5213) is located further downstream at the TN 13 bridge. All canoe liveries are located along the *Tennessee River Tour* and also offer camping.

Duck River (mp 408) Not as pristine as the Buffalo, but still a nice float trip with pastoral scenery and occasional high rocky bluffs. Call River Rat Canoe Rental (931/381-2278) in Columbia.

Fishing

Not being a fisherman myself, my best advice is to talk to the locals. Vernon Summerlin, author of ***Two Dozen Fishin' Holes*** and ***Traveling the Trace***, claims Tennessee has the best fishing opportunities. In Mississippi, Natchez Trace State Park (mp 10), the Ross Barnett Reservoir (mp 105-124), Davis Lake (mp 243), Bay Springs Lake (mp 294), and Tishomingo State Park (mp 303), offer lake fishing for bass, bream, catfish, and crappie. The Tombigbee Waterway (mp

293) and Bear Creek (mp 303 & 313) may be your best bet for river fishing along the Parkway in Mississippi.

You can fish on either side of Pickwick Lake on the Tennessee River in Alabama. In Tennessee, Laurel Hill Lake (mp 373) offers excellent lake fishing and the Buffalo River is teaming with fish (I saw them while I was canoeing!). The Duck River and several large creeks offer additional fishing opportunities.

APPENDICES

PUBLICATIONS

Several books on the Natchez Trace and the Southeast are available at the Parkway Visitor Center bookstore in Tupelo. To order, call 662/840-0580.

Alabama County Maps. AL Dept. of Transportation, Map Sales, 1409 Coliseum Blvd., Rm. R-109, Montgomery, AL 36130. $1.30 each; Detailed road maps which indicate road surfaces—paved, gravel, dirt, etc.

Atlas and Gazetteer. Delorme Mapping, P.O. Box 298, Freeport, ME 04032, (800) 227-1656; $16.95 plus $5.00 shipping. Color topographic maps of each state in the U.S. Gives elevation contour. Shows which areas are forested, cleared, or urban. Recreational information. Shows all back roads but does not specify road surface. Available in some bookstores and bike shops.

Bicycling Middle Tennessee by Ann Richards & Glen Wanner. Pennywell Press, P.O. Box 50624, Nashville, TN 37205; 2002. $15.95 plus $2 shipping. Features rural routes in north central Tennessee including the NTP. Includes greenways and mountain biking. Also available in bike stores and book stores.

Bed, Breakfast, & Bike Mississippi Valley by Dale Lally. Anacus Press, 3943 Meadowbrook Rd. Minneapolis, MN 55426; 2001. $16.95 plus $4 shipping. Features several B&Bs along the Trace and Adventure Cycling's *Great River Route.* Includes info on riding the entire Mississippi Valley and day rides from various B&Bs.

Cycling Tennessee's Highways. TN Dept. of Transportation, Suite 700, James K. Polk Bldg. Nashville, TN 37243-0349, Attn. Bicycle Coord. Free maps of 5 overnight touring routes that are also marked by road signs on state and county roads. The routes are "Cycling to Reelfoot," "Cycling the Tennessee River," "Cycling the Heartland," "Cycling the Highland Rim," and "Cycling the Mountains." "The Heartland" uses the NTP between mp 391 and 429. The *Tennessee River Tour* in this book uses portions of "The River."

Great Rivers Bicycle Route. Adventure Cycling Association, P.O. Box 8308, Missoula, MT 59807, (800) 721-8719; $27.75, $18.75 for members. Set of maps of a bike route from Fargo, North Dakota to Baton Rouge, Louisiana. This route joins the Parkway at TN 50 (mp 408) and continues south through Natchez. Also connects two of Adventure Cycling's trans-continental route, one which run through St. Francisville (90 miles south of Natchez) and the other crosses Kentucky.

Mississippi County Maps. MS Dept. of Transportation, Map Sales, 401 NW St. Jackson, MS 39201. $1.00 each. Detailed road maps which indicate road surfaces—paved, gravel, dirt, etc.

Natchez Trace Parkway. 2680 Natchez Trace Pkwy. Tupelo, MS 38801, (662) 842-1572. Will mail free info on services.

Mississippi River Trail. 777 Walnut Grove Rd. Box 27, Memphis, TN 38120. 901/624-3600 www.mississippiriver-trail.org. Signed bicycle route from St. Louis to New Orleans. Joins NTP near Rocky Springs.

The Natchez Trace; A Pictorial History by James A. Crutchfield. Rutledge Hill Press, 211 7th Ave N. Nashville, TN 37219; 1985. $9.95. Follows the history of the Natchez Trace region from prehistoric times to the modern Parkway. Features numerous historical photographs and drawings.

The Natchez Trace; Two Centuries of Travel by R.C. Gildart. American World Geographic Publishing. P.O. Box 5630, Helena, MT 59604; 1996. $17.95. Follows the history of the Natchez Trace region from prehistoric times to the construction of the Parkway. Features beautiful color photographs.

Tennessee County Maps. TN Dept. of Transportation, Map Sales, Suite 1000, James K. Polk Bldg. 505 Deaderick St., Nashville, TN 37219, (615) 741-2195; $ .50 each. Detailed road maps which indicate road surfaces—paved, gravel, dirt, etc.

Traveling the Natchez Trace by Lori Finley, John Blair Publishers, 1406 Plaza Dr. Winston-Salem, NC 27103; 1995; $12.95. An auto-guide to the Natchez Trace including several towns and historic sites within 50 miles of the Parkway.

Traveling the Trace by Cathy and Vernon Summerlin. Rutledge Hill Press, 211 7th Ave N. Nashville, TN 37219: 1995; $14.95. A Natchez Trace auto-guide including several towns and historic sites within 50 miles of the Parkway.

The Outlaw Years: The History of the Land Pirates of the Natchez Trace by Robert Coates. Pelican Publishing Co. P.O. Box 3110 Gretna, LA 70054; 2002. $7.95. Tales of the heyday of the Natchez Trace. Features stories of outlaws and the hardships endured by the various travelers.

TOURIST INFORMATION

Mississippi
Mississippi Tourism Association, www.mstourism.com
Clinton, (601) 924-5912. www.clintonms.org
Jackson, (601) 960-1891 or (800) 354-7695. www.visitjackson.com
Kosciusko/Attala County, (662) 289-2981. www.kadcorp.org
Natchez, (800) 634-818. www.visitnatchez.com
Port Gibson/Clairborne County. (601) 437-4351.
    www.portgibsononthemississippi.com
Ridgeland, (800) 468-6078. www.visitridgeland.com
Tupelo, (662) 841-6521 or (800) 533-0611. www.tupelo.net
Vicksburg, (601) 636-9421 or (800) 221-3536.
    www.vicksburgcvb.org

Alabama
Florence/Lauderdale, (256) 740-4141 or 888/FLO-TOUR.
    www.visitflorenceal.com

Tennessee
Tennessee Department of Toursim. www.tnvacation.com
Columbia/Maury County, (931) 381-7176 or (800) 381-1865.
Franklin/Williamson County, (615) 791-7554 or (866) 253-9207.
    www.visitwilliamson.com
Hohenwald/Lewis County, (931) 796-4084. www.hohenwaldlewis-
    chamber.com
Nashville, (800) 657-6910 www.visitmusiccity.com
Savannah/Hardin County, (731) 925-818. www.tourhardin-
    county.org
Waynesboro/Wayne County, (931) 722-3277. www.waynecounty-
    chamber.org

NATIONAL PARK SERVICE
Emergency (800) 300-PARK (7275)
Visitor Information (662) 680-4025 or (800) 305-7417. Or write
    Natchez Trace Parkway, 2680 Natchez Trace Pkwy., Tupelo,
    MS 38804. www.nps.gov/natr

Ranger Districts:
Mt. Locust/Natchez (mp 15) (601) 445-4211
Port Gibson (mp 40) (601) 437-5252
Rocky Springs (mp 55) (601) 535-7142
Ridgeland (mp 102) (601) 856-7321
Kosciusko (mp 160) (662) 289-3671

Jeff Busby (mp 193) (662) 387-4365
Dancy (mp 214) (662) 263-5677
Tupelo (mp 266) (662) 680-4025
Colbert Ferry/Cherokee (mp 327) (256) 359-6372
Meriwether Lewis (mp 386) (931) 796-2675
Leipers Fork/Nashville(mp 429) (615) 790-9323

BICYCLE SHOPS

Natchez
Western Auto (bike services)
180 Sgt. Prentiss Dr.
Natchez, MS 39120
(601) 445-4186

Jackson
Indian Cycle Fitness
677 S. Pear Orchard Rd.
Ridgeland, MS 39157
(601) 956-8383

Tupelo

Trails & Treads
1715 McCullough Rd. Ste. F
Tupelo, MS 38801
(662) 690-6620

Bicycle Pacelines
2120 W. Jackson St.
Tupelo, MS 38801
(662) 844-8660

Florence/Sheffield
Bikes Plus
2801 W. Mall Dr.
Florence, AL 35630
(256) 760-9202

Columbia
The Wheel
11 Public Square
Columbia, TN 38401
(931) 381-3225

Franklin

Franklin Bicycle Co.
124 Watson Glen
Franklin, TN 37064
(615) 790-2702

Harpeth Bicycles
1110 Hillsboro Rd.
Franklin, TN 37064
(615) 791-7959

Nashville

Bike Pedlar
2910 West End Ave.
Nashville, TN 37203
(615) 329-2453

Trace Bikes
8400 Hwy 100 (at northern terminus)
Nashville, TN 37221
(615) 646-2485

Cumberland Transit
2807 West End Ave.
Nashville, TN 37203
(615) 327-2453

Gran Fondo
5205 Harding Pk.
Nashville, TN 37205
(615) 354-1090

USEFUL WEBSITES

Bed & Breakfast Online, www.bbonline.com
Bed, Breakfast, & Bike, www.bbbiking.com
Map My Ride, www.mapmyride.com
Mississippi RiverTrail, www.mississippirivertrail.org

COMMERCIAL TOURS

Backroads (800) GOACTIVE. Sag supported B&B tours in the Natchez area and Louisiana.

Black Bear Adventures (888) 339-8687 Sag supported B&B tours from Jackson to Natchez and from Nashville to Tupelo. Can also arrange custom tours.

Classic Adventures (800) 777-8090. Sag supported B&B tours from Jackson to Natchez via Vicksburg in the fall and spring.

Natchez Trace Bed & Breakfast Reservation Service (800) 377-2770, www.natcheztracetravel.com. Will book accomodations along the Trace. Assists in arranging transportation to and from the airport. Also arranges shuttles to B&Bs located several miles off the Parkway.

For updates and inquiries about traveling the Natchez Trace, e-mail glen.wanner@vanderbilt.edu

Additional copies of this book and
Bicycling Middle Tennessee *may be obtained by sending check or money order to:*

Pennywell Press
P.O. Box 50624
Nashville, TN 37205

Please enclose $15.95 per book
plus $2 for shipping/handling.

Distributed to the book trade by:
John F. Blair Publishers
1406 Plaza Dr.
Winston-Salem, NC 27103